# Window Treatments with Style

WINDOW TREATMENTS WITH STYLE.
All rights reserved. For information, address St. Martin's Press,
175 Fifth Avenue, New York, N.Y. 10010.

www.stmartins.com

Copyright © 2015 RotoVision SA
www.rotovision.com

The written instructions, photographs, designs, patterns, and projects
in this volume are intended for personal use of the reader and may be
reproduced for that purpose only.

Library of Congress Cataloging-in-Publication Data Available Upon Request

ISBN: 978-1-250-05209-4

First U.S. Edition: February 2015

10 9 8 7 6 5 4 3 2 1

Publisher: Mark Searle
Editorial Director: Isheeta Mustafi
Commissioning Editor: Jacqeuline Ford
Editor: Diane Leyman
Assistant Editor: Tamsin Richardson
Book layout: Emma Atkinson
Photographer: Alison Stevens
Cover design: Michelle Rowlandson
Illustrations: Peters & Zabransky and Rob Brandt

Printed and bound in China

Cover image credits:
Front cover (clockwise from top left): Charlotte
Rivers/Lottie Loves; Lara Cameron/Ink & Spindle;
Lara Cameron/Ink & Spindle; Lisa Barrett/Tango
& James; Lara Cameron/Ink & Spindle; Linda
Dresselhaus/Itsy Bits and Pieces.
Back cover (left to right): Nancy Purvis/Owen's
Olivia; Dovilé Cavina/Lovely Home Idea.

# Window Treatments with Style

Fresh Ideas and Techniques for Upstyling Your Windows

Hannah Stanton

ST. MARTIN'S GRIFFIN
NEW YORK

# Contents

**Opposite:** Melissa Braedley/Living Beautifully DIY

# SECTION 3
## Resources

# Introduction

Writing this book gave me an excuse to catch up with all the makers out there. I was blown away by the many exciting curtain and blinds projects posted online. How great it is that we can share the things we make and love with the world! As well as showcasing new talent, the internet is a fantastic resource for inspiration, project tips, and ideas. The images and case studies in this book feature a small selection of those projects.

Buying huge quantities of fabric and paying a professional can often blow an interiors budget out of the water and put the brakes on you realizing your window treatment dreams. While the thought of making your own curtains and blinds can feel daunting, the process is surprisingly simple. Even the most inexperienced sewer can tackle the world of window treatments. Some of the most effective projects I've seen have been the simplest, involving drop cloths, curtain clips, stencils, and dyes.

In this book I guide you through the maze of fabric, color, pattern, and texture choices, with tutorials that can be completed using fairly basic tools. Enjoy the designing and making process! Consider customizing store-bought curtains and blinds. Add to them, take them apart, paint, and embellish. If you are bitten by the bug, take it to the next level and sign up for a class. Most of all, have fun!

*Hannah Stanton*

**Opposite:** Linda Weinstein/Calling It Home

# SECTION 1

## Introductory Basics

# CHAPTER 1
## Tools and Materials
# Overview

I absolutely love tools, and if money and space
were no object, my collection would be vast!
Thankfully, curtain making has quite simple
and inexpensive tool requirements, and a sewing
machine will likely be your largest outlay. If you're
new to curtain making or sewing I'd suggest
making friends with your local haberdasher—
nothing beats experience when it comes to the
nuances of particular sewing machine brands.
When it comes to scissors, my advice is to arm
yourself with the best you can afford, and look
after them—even a short fall from a chair can
damage blades.

The materials required for your projects will
depend on the situation and your vision. There's
a wealth of choices, whether it's heading tapes or
poles and tracks. When it comes to curtain rods,
I've even seen tree branches and copper pipe
utilized. Have some fun and explore the options!

**Previous page:** Lara Cameron/Ink & Spindle
**Opposite:** Photo by Sherry Heck

# Measuring and Marking Tools

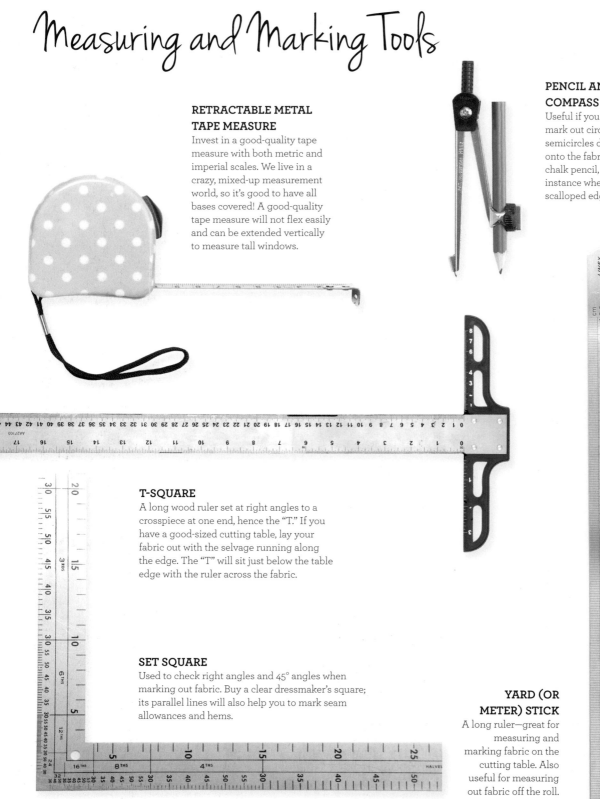

### RETRACTABLE METAL TAPE MEASURE

Invest in a good-quality tape measure with both metric and imperial scales. We live in a crazy, mixed-up measurement world, so it's good to have all bases covered! A good-quality tape measure will not flex easily and can be extended vertically to measure tall windows.

### PENCIL AND COMPASS

Useful if you need to mark out circles or semicircles directly onto the fabric with a chalk pencil, for instance when making scalloped edges.

### T-SQUARE

A long wood ruler set at right angles to a crosspiece at one end, hence the "T." If you have a good-sized cutting table, lay your fabric out with the selvage running along the edge. The "T" will sit just below the table edge with the ruler across the fabric.

### SET SQUARE

Used to check right angles and 45° angles when marking out fabric. Buy a clear dressmaker's square; its parallel lines will also help you to mark seam allowances and hems.

### YARD (OR METER) STICK

A long ruler—great for measuring and marking fabric on the cutting table. Also useful for measuring out fabric off the roll.

### WATER-SOLUBLE MARKERS AND PENCILS

More expensive than chalk, but finer and a bit easier to use. Always do a test to make sure the marks wash out of the fabric you are using.

### CALCULATOR

As we all know, it's used for working out calculations. You can use your brain, but it's good practice to double-check. Measure twice, cut once—it really is worth checking that all the dimensions you take from the window add up.

### TAILOR'S CHALK

Tailor's chalk comes in various shapes and sizes, and in colors to contrast with any fabric. The advantage of tailor's chalk is that marks can be easily brushed or washed off fabric.

### STEPLADDER

It might sound strange, but if you are measuring down from a curtain pole, it really helps to be at eye level with it. As your health and safety adviser, I'd say not to stand on stools and chairs—it just isn't safe!

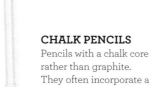

### CHALK PENCILS

Pencils with a chalk core rather than graphite. They often incorporate a brush at one end to easily remove marks once they are no longer needed.

### FRENCH CURVE

A plastic template with all sorts of curves cut into it. Useful if you need to draw a smooth curve that isn't part of a circle.

### CHALK WHEEL

A modern variation on traditional tailor's chalk; a bit like a tiny road marker. Run the wheel along the fabric and it leaves behind a chalk line—without getting your hands dirty.

# Cutting and Pressing Tools

### SEAM RIPPERS

A great and sometimes necessary tool to have for reopening seams that have gone wrong! One of my favorite tools.

### DRESSMAKING SCISSORS

Similar to fabric shears, but typically lighter and shorter. Useful for cutting gentle curves and in more general work but, like fabric shears, they should only ever be used for cutting fabric.

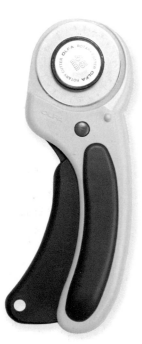

### ROTARY CUTTERS

Usually used in quilting, rotary cutters take a bit of getting used to but are a really useful tool for cutting fast and accurately, as the fabric stays flat to the cutting surface. Be careful and always use with a cutting mat!

### PINKING SHEARS

These shears have notched blades so that they cut a zigzag line, which is useful when trimming raw seam edges to prevent fraying.

## POINT TURNER

Point turners are basically small, pointed, flat pieces of plastic or wood—really useful when turning out and pressing corners and seams.

## THREAD SNIPS

Typically small snips without handles, used for snipping thread ends. They are also useful for cutting small curves and corners and should always be kept on hand next to your sewing machine.

## PRESSING CLOTH

When ironing on the face of any fabric it is always best to use a pressing cloth—it will prevent damage to delicate fabrics and avoid a shine on heavier ones. Silk organza is ideal, as it can withstand high temperatures and, being translucent, can aid visibility.

## FABRIC SHEARS

Heavy, metal fabric cutting scissors designed with handles that angle upward when the lower blade is on a flat surface. This allows you to cut fabric accurately without lifting it far from the cutting surface.

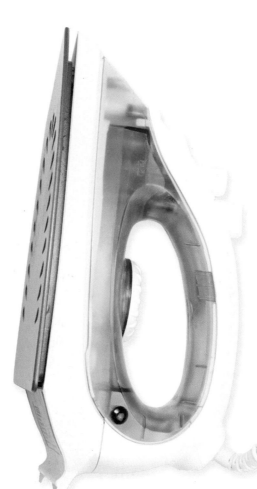

## IRON

As with any sewing project, curtain and blind making requires a good-quality steam iron. Always fill the reservoir with distilled water, especially if you live in an area with hard water.

# Fabrics for Lining

## BLACKOUT LINING

A lining that blocks out light and often provides additional thermal insulation. Typically made by applying alternate coats of white and black foam to a polycotton fabric, hence the terms "2-pass" and "3-pass" that you often see when buying blackout fabric. Alternatively, blackout can be achieved by the traditional French method, where two interlinings of black fabric and a flannel layer are sewn between the visible face and lining fabrics.

## COTTON SATEEN

The most common curtain lining. Cotton sateen is economical and often Sanforized, which is a preshrinking process that reduces movement after washing or ironing.

## INTERLININGS

Interlinings are additional linings layered in between the visible face and lining fabrics. Interlinings can aid insulation from sound, cold and light, but are most commonly used to create fuller, more sumptuous curtains.

## INTERFACING

Interfacings are fabrics sewn or ironed into curtain headers and seams to provide additional stiffness. They are particularly useful for curtain headers where heading tape is not being used.

# Sundries

## THREAD

There are plenty of debates about the merits of various thread types, but here are the basics: mercerized (a process that strengthens and adds luster) cotton threads are perfect for hand sewing, but polycotton thread is best for machine sewing. Use a good-quality thread to avoid furring up your machine.

## TRIMMINGS

There is a huge range of fabric trimmings available in stores and online, and you can also make your own. They can be used to customize and accessorize your curtains.

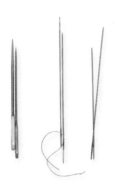

## PINS

There are a variety of pins available for different applications. Standard dressmaking pins are fine for curtain making.

## NEEDLES

Needles can be straight or curved and come in a variety of weights, lengths, and eye sizes. Use fine needles for fine fabrics and larger eyes for heavier threads.

## HEADING TAPES

Heading tapes are generally made from cotton or polycotton. They stiffen the head of your curtains and allow curtain hooks to be attached to strings or woven pockets. There are a wide variety available for different weights of fabric and curtain types.

# Curtain Poles and Rods

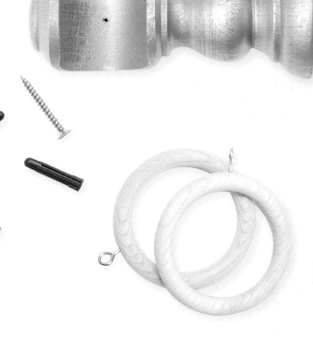

### CURTAIN ROD SUPPORTS AND BRACKETS

Supports and brackets should generally be the same finish as your pole. They are attached to the wall to hold the ends and center of the pole. The last ring on the curtain will be placed on the finial side of the bracket. This will hold the curtains in place when they are drawn. Wide and bay windows will need intermediate supports that do not stop the curtain from drawing. These are referred to as "passing" brackets and are used with passing rings.

### CURTAIN RINGS

A curtain ring is a simple ring with an eyelet at the base to hang the curtain hook. Whichever pole system you choose, it will have a matching curtain ring that works with it. This is of particular importance if using passing brackets, as they need to work together.

### CURTAIN POLES

Curtain poles are available in many sizes, materials, and lengths. They come in standard sizes, enabling you to mix and match poles, finials, rings, and brackets to create the pole system of your choice. If you have bay windows in your house, flexible pole joiners are available. If you're friendly with a local metalworker, you can have yours custom-shaped.

### CURTAIN ROD FINIALS

Finials are available in all shapes and sizes to match, contrast, or complement your chosen pole. As well as stopping the curtains falling off the end, they are also good for adding visual interest to the pole.

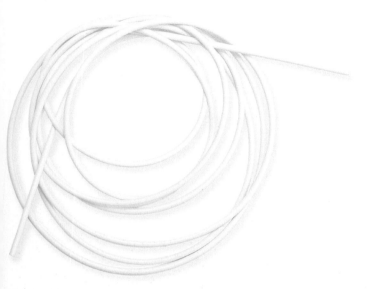

### SPRING WIRE

Rarely seen these days, plastic-coated curtain spring wire is simply hung onto eyelets that are screwed into the timber of a window frame. It is traditionally used to hang net curtains and to provide privacy without blocking light, but can also be used to hang muslin or other sheer fabrics.

### BLIND PULL

This is a toggle used to finish the end of a blind or curtain cord. It really can be anything with a hole running through it, but try to choose something that adds a decorative element to your window treatment.

### TENSION ROD

This is a simple "quick fix" solution for hanging curtains in a window recess. It is a simple pole that extends and holds itself in place through tension rather than traditional fixings.

### CURTAIN HOOKS

Available in plastic or metal, curtain hooks are the connection between the curtain ring and the curtain. They allow you to hook and unhook the curtains without removing the rings from the pole.

### CORD HOOK

A simple hook or cleat used to hold a blind or curtain cord neatly in the desired position.

### CURTAIN TRACKS

Curtain tracks are typically made in plastic, aluminum, or steel. Which type to use depends principally on the weight of the curtains. There are many systems on the market, usually with a pulley style to allow curtains to be retracted using cords at the ends of the rail. Other systems provide parallel rails, allowing sheer curtains to be hung behind heavier ones. Plastic systems are often designed to be flexible to account for bay windows.

# CHAPTER 2

## Choosing Fabrics

# Overview

Fabric is so enticing. I find myself helplessly drawn to vivid colors and bold patterns, leaving me feeling like a giddy, love-struck teenager! I have an irresistible urge to handle every piece of fabric that lands in front of me, exploring the various textures. To some, the thought of drowning in a sea of fabric bolts is terrifying, but the best way to approach fabric shopping is to plan ahead. Having a vision for your room and an idea of how you want your curtains or blinds to look will help manage the choices. There are always rules when it comes to color and pattern, but if you have an alternative vision, run with it!

**Opposite:** Gap Interiors/Spike Powell

# Fabric Characteristics

## COTTON

Cotton is probably the most commonly found fabric in the home, and is a popular choice for all manner of soft furnishing projects. It's easy to look after and can be incredibly durable. There are many grades of cotton, so it can be light or heavyweight. It is harvested from the cotton plant, mainly in the USA, North Africa, and India.

## CHINTZ

Modern chintz is typically a glazed woven fabric with a shiny finish, often featuring large flower repeats. Chintz was originally produced in India during the 1600s using woodblock printing methods. These fabrics were imported to Europe where they became immensely popular as textiles for bed linen and draperies. The glaze effect given to chintz affects the fabric drape and can give a sharp, more formal look to curtains.

## TICKING

Ticking is produced with a bed-tick, twill, or herringbone weave. The vintage varieties are much more tightly woven than modern versions, and you'll often see it used in mattresses, feather pillows, etc. A classic feature of ticking is the pinstripe pattern. Originally, the pattern would have only been produced with indigo blue stripes, but nowadays it is available in a variety of colors and patterns.

## TOILE DE JOUY

Toile fabrics originated in Ireland in the 1700s and became popular in England and France, where they were produced in the town of Jouy-en-Josas. The term "toile de Jouy" was the name given to fabric toiles featuring scenes from everyday life, classically from the French countryside. Traditionally, toiles are printed in a single color on either white or off-white backgrounds.

## SHEERS

Is the collective name for semitransparent fabric. In curtain making, sheers are usually white, off-white, or cream, and are sometimes embellished with embroidery. Sheer curtains are used where you want to let light in but retain an element of privacy.

## VOILE

Voile is a sheer, lightweight woven fabric, great for creating a romantic feel. This fabric offers privacy during the day while also allowing light to stream into a room. Voiles can be made from cotton or a blend of linen or polyester.

## NET

Netting is a low-cost window treatment. Net curtains were originally made from cotton or silk lace, but few outlets offer this due to the price. It is now more commonly made from polyester and can be patterned or plain.

## ORGANZA

Organza is a sheer fabric traditionally made from silk, commonly used for bridal wear. There are many different qualities of organza available dependent on where they are produced. The most expensive are woven in France and Italy. The more synthetic versions made from viscose and acetate are used in curtain making.

# WOOL

Wool is incredibly hardwearing, so is often used to furnish public spaces, such as galleries and theaters. The wool fiber is not easily crushed, so is plump and luxurious in feel. It is probably one of the only fabrics to combine luxury with a high resistance to wear. It is naturally protected from staining and is also ecologically sound.

## PLAID

Plaid, or tartan, is a woolen fabric primarily associated with Scotland. The Highland tartans were associated with particular regions or clan. Plaids are plain-woven.

## TWEED

Tweed is generally of a twill weave with a herringbone or check pattern. Traditionally, tweed was used for outdoor clothing, but it looks great for all sorts of soft furnishing projects. It can sometimes be pretty coarse to the touch, but is moisture resistant and highly durable. A famous product is Harris Tweed, made in the Outer Hebrides in Scotland.

## FELT

Felt is made by adding water to layers of woolen fibers. As you agitate and add heat, the fibers become entangled and start to shrink and become compacted. Felts are available in an array of colors and thicknesses and can also be made at home—although making floor-length curtains could be a step too far! It has the added benefit of not fraying, but does have a tendency to pill. Worldwide suppliers of good-quality upholstery felt are Kvadrat and Camira.

# DEEP PILE

Refers to the raised loops or strands of yarn in a fabric. The simplest pile construction is the double-cloth method, where two cloths are woven face-to-face with a separate pile yarn joining them. The extra yarn is then cut, separating the two pieces of fabric. The pile is then trimmed and brushed. The color of pile fabrics will change depending on how the light hits them.

## VELVET

Velvet has been used in soft furnishings for centuries. It was traditionally made from natural fibers of silk and cotton. Today, there are also synthetic variants such as polyester and nylon, some of which are cheaper and can look and feel like they are of a low quality. The quality is also determined by the density of the tufts and quality of the backing. Traditionally, you would make curtains with the pile running down the curtain; brushing down against the pile means it is susceptible to gathering more dust.

## CHENILLE

Chenille, the French word for "caterpillar," is a very soft and thick-pile fabric. And yes, it does look a bit like a caterpillar! Chenille is made by twisting long and short strands of yarn together. The short yarns then stand away from the long, giving a fuzzy, caterpillar-like appearance. It's these exposed strands that catch the light from many angles, giving chenille an almost iridescent look. The yarn can be silk, cotton, wool, or manmade, such as rayon or olefin. It is a durable fabric, but has a tendency to fray.

## CORDUROY

Corduroy is a ribbed pile fabric. Extra weft yarns float over a number of warp yarns, which are then cut and brushed to produce the "cord" effect. It is a highly durable fabric commonly associated with clothing, often used for pants, jackets, and shirts. The width of the cord is referred to as the size of the "wale." The lower the wale number, the thicker the cord. The cords bounce light around a room, so this is a great fabric for adding texture.

## SILK

Silk is a natural, protein-based fiber produced by silkworms. It is a very delicate fabric with a luxurious look and feel. It can, however, stain easily and in some cases may need specialist care. It is available in various weights and colors.

## BROCADE

Brocade is a luxurious-looking fabric with a slightly raised, embroidery-like design. Traditionally, brocade was made with colored silks, but synthetic varieties are also available today—with obvious price differences! Brocade has an additional weft thread. This thread is nonstructural, and gives the appearance that the weave is embroidered on. Turn the fabric over and you'll see floating threads. Brocade frays easily, so take care.

## DAMASK

Damask is a patterned fabric traditionally woven in silk. It is also available in wool, linen, cotton, and synthetic fibers, and is traditionally monochrome. The pattern, usually floral, is created with the weft yarns during the weaving process, the pattern becoming visible as the light hits it. The name derives from the city of Damascus, where the fabric was produced and traded in the Middle Ages.

Damask is most suited to elegant, traditional-style curtains. There are modern colorways available that have a more contemporary feel. Generally, damask works well on floor-length curtains.

## MOIRÉ

Moiré is more often than not a silk-based fabric, but it can also be cotton-based. Its watermark-like appearance is created in the finishing process. The fabric is folded and passed under engraved rollers at a high temperature and pressure. It is then run through another set of rollers that polish the surface, making the fabric smoother and more lustrous. This process is referred to as calendering. The overall effect gives the fabric a textured appearance. To the touch, moiré is flat. Today moiré is often made using manmade fibers.

## WOVEN AND SPECIALTY FABRICS

### LINEN

Linen is a bast fiber made from the flax plant. It is used in many different ways. It's a wearable fabric that's great for keeping cool in, and was also used to wrap up mummies in ancient Egypt. More recently, the word "linen" has been used as a collective term for bath, table, and kitchen textiles. Linen alone tends to crease very easily and so is often mixed with other fibers to create a "linen union," where it then excels as a fabric and creases less.

### HEMP

Camira's "Second Nature" range includes a 40/60% hemp and wool mix. The hemp is grown from the plants in the cannabis genus. It's a bast fiber plant like flax and jute—the textile fiber occurs just inside the outer bark. The Camira hemp is grown in the UK as an agricultural crop under license from the government on farms in Leicestershire and is available for purchase worldwide.

### FAUX SUEDE

Faux suede is popular in soft furnishings. It is used in furniture coverings as well as curtains, cushions, and throws. It has a soft handle and is made from 100% polyester, which means it's very durable. As the name suggests, faux suede is made to mimic the look of regular suede. It is a great alternative if you love the feel of suede but want to avoid using products derived from animals. Faux suede changes color when you rub it in different directions. The manufacturer runs a coarse brush over the top of the fabric to create a matted, fuzzy texture.

**Opposite:** Gap Interiors/Tria Giovan

| | MOST SUITED TO | PROS | CONS |
|---|---|---|---|
| **COTTON** | • Great for almost any soft furnishing project | • Inexpensive<br>• Durable<br>• Holds color well<br>• Good resistance to pilling<br>• Easy to handle | • Creases easily<br>• Can fade after prolonged exposure to sunlight<br>• Machine washing can change the body of the fabric (so test-wash a sample) |
| **SHEERS** | • Elegant window treatments<br>• Creating privacy, full coverage of windows, and letting in light | • Hides an unsightly view while allowing light to flood in<br>• Drapes well<br>• Crease resistant<br>• As it's sheer you don't need to worry about lining | • Tricky to clean<br>• Highly flammable<br>• Not great for heat insulation<br>• Difficult to cut and work with because of the sheer structure, and sometimes wider than average widths |
| **WOOL** | • Curtains in cold climates | • Warm<br>• Holds its shape well<br>• Doesn't crease<br>• Highly flame-resistant<br>• Does not attract dirt<br>• Antistatic<br>• Hardwearing<br>• Fantastic color range (as wool absorbs dyes well) | • Attracts moths<br>• May need professional cleaning |
| **DEEP PILE** | • Curtains<br>• Often used for swags and tails | • Soft to the touch<br>• Luxurious<br>• Great for drafty windows | • Very heavy, which makes it a little tricky to work with<br>• Marks easily<br>• You can't wrap the finished curtains to create folds, as the velvet will mark<br>• Attracts moths<br>• Can be expensive, depending on the blend |

| DURABILITY | TIPS FOR WORKING WITH | CLEANING AND CARE | ALLERGY INFO |
|---|---|---|---|
| • Highly durable | • Has good give and is an easy textile to work with<br>• Creases easily, so always keep on the roll when not in use | • Remove stains with warm water and a little neutral soap<br>• Rinse with clean water<br>• Can be protected with a stain guard | • Generally hypoallergenic |
| • Quite durable | • Use a stabilizer such as tissue paper when stitching to prevent movement<br>• Use a walking foot attachment if possible<br>• Hold the fabric in place with clamps when cutting out, as it can be slippery<br>• It's best to cut out fabrics on a large cutting table<br>• Use a continuous length of weight for the bottom of the curtain, one that is specifically designed for sheers | • Lightly vacuum to remove any loose dirt<br>• Generally dry-clean<br>• Some marks can be washed, but be aware that some good-quality voiles have dressings that will wash away and leave the fabric limp | |
| • Medium durability | • Wool (apart from felt) tends to fray easily, so zigzag or overlock stitch any raw edges | • Wool is prone to shrinking and felting, so wash gently or dry-clean | • Raw wool is naturally hypoallergenic |
| • Not very durable | • Attach a wand on the leading-edge curtain ring so that you don't need to touch the curtains when opening<br>• Put a slight zigzag in your stitch as you sew a seam to alleviate pulling<br>• Keep on the roll when not in use and avoid folding<br>• Where possible, do not cut off selvages when joining pieces—they will help to reduce slippage of the fabric when stitching<br>• Do not attempt at any stage to iron velvet, as this will damage the pile<br>• Use a walking foot when sewing to reduce slippage | • Vacuum regularly<br>• Steam clean | |

|  |  | MOST SUITED TO | PROS | CONS |
|---|---|---|---|---|
| **SILK** | | • Elegant window treatments<br>• Creating privacy, full coverage of windows, and letting in light | • Crease resistant<br>• Silk drapes well and when combined with interlining creates a rich, luxurious look<br>• Silk takes dye very well, hence the range of vibrant colors | • Sunlight can rot silk<br>• Color fades easily<br>• Tricky to clean<br>• Highly flammable<br>• Difficult to cut and work with because of its sheer structure, and sometimes comes in wider than average widths<br>• Expensive |
| **LINEN** | | • A casual-style window treatment<br>• Good in hot climates as it feels cool to the touch<br>• Curtains and pelmets | • Does not shed lint<br>• Strong fiber<br>• Antistatic<br>• Drapes well | • Creases easily<br>• Likely to shrink |
| **HEMP** | | • Curtains and blinds<br>• Upholstery | • Soft to the touch<br>• Inherently flame-retardant<br>• Sustainable fabric<br>• Fast growing without the use of chemicals<br>• Available in many colors | • Liable to fray |
| **FAUX SUEDE** | | • Full-length curtains | • Easy to wash<br>• Drapes well<br>• A good insulator<br>• Doesn't fray<br>• Available in different weights<br>• Adds a texture to the room<br>• Available in a range of colors | • Not suitable to use with curtain wires or tension rods |

| DURABILITY | TIPS FOR WORKING WITH | CLEANING AND CARE | ALLERGY INFO |
|---|---|---|---|
| • Quite durable | • Line silk curtains, as sunlight can rot the silk<br>• Use a stabilizer such as tissue paper when stitching to prevent movement<br>• Use a walking foot attachment if possible<br>• Hold the fabric in place with clamps when cutting out, as it can be slippery<br>• It's best to cut out fabrics on a large cutting table<br>• Use a continuous length of weight specifically designed for sheers for the bottom of the curtain | • Silk will most likely require specialist cleaning, so refer to instructions from the supplier<br>• Lightly vacuum to remove any loose dirt<br>• Generally dry-clean<br>• Water will leave marks on silk<br>• Some marks can be washed, but be aware that some good-quality silks have dressings that will wash away and leave the fabric limp | • Silk has been known to bring on asthma and allergic rhinitis |
| • Highly durable | • Creases easily, so always keep on the roll when not in use<br>• Linen is often produced with a print for furnishing fabrics, so check that the pattern has been printed straight. Your fabric may be expensive, but that doesn't always guarantee perfection. | • Brush or gently vacuum<br>• Dry-clean | |
| • Durable | • Can fray so serge cut edges | • Use a soft brush to remove dirt<br>• Can also be lightly vacuumed<br>• Do not wash as it is likely to shrink | |
| • Durable | • It can be difficult to tell the right from wrong side, but the right side has more of an even distribution of color<br>• If you do decide to hem the curtain, only make a single fold<br>• Iron with a press cloth and set the temperature for polyester<br>• Make sure the nap runs in the same direction on any widths or panels. Indicate the direction using tailor's chalk on the reverse of the fabric | • Occasionally wipe down with a damp cloth<br>• Can also be dusted<br>• Use a soap to lift any stains | |

# Color Schemes

One of the most important decisions you'll need to make when it comes to curtains is color. Color has the power to make you feel warm, cold, happy, or even hungry. Used incorrectly, color may just drive you mad. Don't be scared—be bold, but stick to some basic rules.

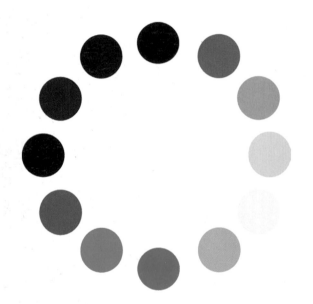

## COLOR WHEEL

It's hard to talk about color without mentioning the color wheel. Having a basic understanding of how the wheel works will really help inform your decisions when choosing colors for your curtains and blinds.

The color wheel starts with the primaries—blue, red, and yellow—and every other color is a mixture of these three. The secondary colors sit between the primaries and are the colors made when the primaries are combined. Tertiary colors are combinations of a primary and a secondary color.

Colors that sit opposite each other on the color wheel are complementary—blue and orange, and yellow and purple. While they work well together, the contrast can be overwhelming if used in large color blocks. Colors that sit

next to each other on the wheel and are of the same hue are referred to as analogous—yellow, yellow-green, and green, for example. These colors work well together because they are harmonious.

The color wheel can also be divided into cold and warm colors. Greens, blues, and purples feel colder than the yellow, orange, and red spectrum.

## CHOOSING COLOR

Whether you're transforming a room as a whole or just updating your window treatments, you need to work within a color palette. If you have an existing piece of furniture already in situ, use the color of this as the starting point for your palette.

If transforming a room from scratch and seeking inspiration, the best place to start is the internet. There are a plethora of online blogs, interiors magazines, and tools for saving to online scrapbooks. Although a valuable resource, wading through pages of images can be overwhelming. Stay focused and keep your own project in mind. Buying large quantities of expensive fabric for your curtains is a serious investment.

## ATMOSPHERE

What mood do you want to create? Do you have a living room that needs to feel warm and comforting? Or an office space that needs to feel fresh and lively? The colors you choose, along with texture and pattern, will be important in setting the mood. Also think about light. If the room spends most of the day in darkness, brighter colors and reflective textures will bounce light around the space. Cool colors can have the effect of opening out a room and creating a more spacious environment. A dark color palette can be sophisticated and atmospheric. Test color by painting samples onto large pieces of paper and then position at different points in the room, such as next to and opposite the window. Keep in place as the day becomes night. Remember, color can change dramatically depending on the type of light that hits it.

## COLOR PALETTE

Colors don't necessarily need to match, but you should aim for an element of cohesion. Make a plan for the room as a whole. Think about the relationship between the floor, the walls, the curtains, and the furniture. Think about balance.

When I'm working on a color scheme, I like to keep the two main colors either harmonious or tonally similar. The third I make complementary, from the opposite side of the color wheel. I do, however, tend to keep the bold contrast color to a large ornament or rug.

Take care when using purely complementary colors in your scheme, as sometimes the contrast can be too great. It's good to be bold with color, but also have areas in the room that give your eyes a rest! You may like the idea of a blue wall with orange curtains, but maybe keep the orange to the trim or lining, for the occasional flash of color. Having said all that, the rules can of course be broken!

## COLOR FADE

It's unavoidable that curtains will fade in sunlight. Bright pinks, blues, and greens are the most vulnerable. If using these colors, use linings or a blind as a filter for the light.

**Right:** Amelia Warren/House Pretty Blog

# Weight and Drape

You've worked out the colors for your room scheme and found the perfect patterned fabric, but does it have the right weight and drape for your chosen window treatment?

## WHAT'S THE DIFFERENCE?

The weight of a fabric is an easy concept to grasp. You can work out whether a fabric is heavy or light just by picking it up and handling it. Assessing the drape of a fabric is a little trickier, and drape should not be confused with weight—there is no direct correlation between the two. What's more important is the fabric structure. How fluid does it feel in your hand, for example?

## HOW TO CHECK FOR WEIGHT AND DRAPE

If you are unsure about the drape, go to a fabric showroom and hold up a large sample of the fabric you are considering. Make soft folds, replicating your finished curtain when pulled back. Does it splay out or flare like an A-line skirt, or do the folds continue down the length? If you are limited to buying your fabrics online, maybe ask for some samples to be sent or contact someone to see if they can help.

While you can make fabric stiffer by adding interfacing or interlining, you can't make a stiff fabric more drapey, so take the time to check before you buy.

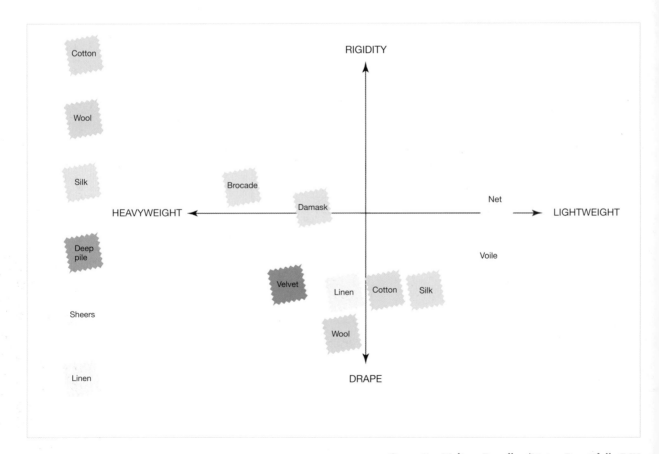

**Opposite:** Melissa Braedley/Living Beautifully DIY

# Pattern and Texture

Using patterned fabric can instantly inject personality into a room. As with color, pattern has the power to play with your emotions. With so much choice, the process of finding the right pattern can be quite overwhelming. Walking into a fabric store can send a rush of endorphins to some, and bring paralyzed trauma to others. If it's the latter, then it's good to visit a fabric store with a list of "wants" so that you feel prepared. A checklist will include color, style, and size of pattern, as well as the weight and type of fabric.

## PATTERN STYLES

Whether printed, woven, or embroidered, there are many pattern styles to consider. As well as the obvious squares, circles, and triangles, the geometric family also includes any abstracted pattern such as paisleys. Anything that isn't figurative sits under this banner. As the name suggests, florals are those with flowers in the pattern, and are one of the most common styles of fabric. Any other pattern that incorporates figurative images is known as a conversational motif. A classic example is toile de Jouy, an eighteenth-century French fabric that is still very much in fashion. Toiles feature scenes from everyday life, classically from the French countryside. More recent incarnations feature modern scenes of cityscapes. Other conversational motifs can include objects, such as children's fabrics featuring robots, dinosaurs, toys, etc.

## FASHION

All patterns change with the seasons, which brings us to fashion. While fashion influences us all, I would suggest avoiding this year or season's defining print. Remember, you're not going to be changing your curtains every year, so don't choose a fabric that will immediately date your room. Also consider the appropriateness of your fabric to your home. Unless you're trying to be deliberately witty, chintzy florals may look out of place in a modern apartment.

## PRINTED PATTERNS

Commonly, pattern is screen-printed onto fabric. A screen is made from a metal or wooden frame with one side covered in a woven mesh. A photosensitive medium is spread across the mesh and an image is exposed onto it. Once the medium is washed away from the screen, you are left with open areas for the ink to pass through. Each color in a design is printed using a separate screen. If you're thinking about printing your own fabric, take this into consideration, as it will greatly increase your setup costs. Your design will need to be color-separated with a screen exposed for each.

Digital printing has opened the door to more elaborate fabric designs. Much like your home printer, a whole spectrum of color is achievable. Various fabric weights can be printed, from simple cottons to silks and even velvet. Having your own fabric digitally printed is also pretty easy. There are companies who will set up your artwork for print if you are a computer novice.

## WOVEN PATTERNS

Pattern is not just restricted to flat cotton, but can also be created in the weave. Think tartan, tweed, brocade, and damask. The basic principles of weaving can be traced back more than 9,000 years. In a nutshell, two distinct sets of yarns are interlaced at right angles to make a fabric. By combining different colored yarns, complex or simple patterns can be created. Over the centuries, weaving technology has progressed from hand to increasingly complex mechanized looms. The most famous and first programmable loom was the jacquard, invented in the 1800s.

## HAND-EMBROIDERED PATTERNS

A much more labor-intensive pattern-making process is hand embroidery. Traditional embroidery employs a simple needle and thread, although embellishments such as beads, pearls, and sequins are also common. Crewel is a system of chain stitching and French knots using strong and fine woolen thread, and can be used to embellish curtains. Care must be taken when cleaning embroidered fabric, so take this into consideration.

Other techniques you may come across are flocking and embossing. Flocking has a soft, velvet-like texture, and is produced when finely cut fibers stick to an adhesive. Gaufrage is the term given to embossed velvet, where a pattern is applied using heat.

## SMALL PATTERNS

From a distance, a small pattern can look like it has texture. The general rule is that a small pattern will make a small room feel larger, but in a large room the pattern can disappear. I like a combination of print sizes in a room, but they all need to connect somehow. Look for unity in color or style.

## LARGE PATTERNS

If the room is large you can get away with bold patterns. In small rooms, a large pattern can feel overwhelming, and even make the room seem smaller.

## STRIPES

More rules! The main rule with stripes is that vertical stripes will make the room feel taller and horizontal stripes will make the room feel wider. I do, however, think thin vertical stripes can also appear to widen a room.

## COLOR

More often than not, a patterned fabric will come in various colorways. This greatly increases your choices, especially if there is already a wealth of color in the room. Some sassy fabric producers will also group patterns and colorways together for you. Two or three different fabrics are designed as a set and grouped into six or more colorways. If you look closely, you'll see a common thread that holds the patterns together. Use the color of larger pieces, such as a sofa, carpet, or rug as your starting point. However, try to limit the color palette. Too many colors in one place can be distracting. It might be perfect for a child's room, but perhaps not for the relaxing areas of your home.

## TEXTURES

I love texture. I think I'm not alone when I say that my first instinct is to reach out and hold a fabric in my hands. You're probably not going to be touching curtains or blinds that often, but like pattern, texture can be appreciated from afar. Texture can be coarse like linen or soft like chenille or velvet. The construction of the fabric can create areas of light and dark, adding depth and movement. Some woven fabrics, such as damask, have a slightly embossed texture. Napped fabrics like velvet, chenille, or corduroy change in feel and color when stroked in different directions. Silks not only feel luxurious, they also bounce light around the room, and are great used in dark areas. Lace or netting does have a bad rap—for some they conjure images of grandma's yellowing kitchen curtains—but they do have their moments in the sun, and there are now many modern designs available.

# Function and Form

Unless your curtains and blinds are purely decorative, it is likely they will need to perform a particular function. You may have a heavily swagged window treatment in mind, but how suitable is it for your steamy bathroom? From the start, you will need to focus on the important functionality issues. Make a checklist of needs. Your overriding factor may be budget, forcing you to make compromises, but functionality shouldn't be one of them. Do, however, go for the best quality of fabric your budget will allow.

## FUNCTION

### WARMTH

I love an old house rich in character and history. These can, however, be full of problems, one being their tendency to move, creating drafty gaps around windows and doors. Window renovation can be costly, and if you're renting, the decision is out of your hands. With curtains and blinds, the addition of lining and interlining, or simply choosing the right fabric, will really help with insulation. Velvet is a great choice for warmth, but it can also be somewhat harsh on the wallet, so look around for jacquard or faux suede. If your weather changes dramatically from season to season, think about making two sets of curtains on a double track or rail. Position the insulating curtain on the window side in winter and remove during the summer months. Lightweight fabrics will not hang so well with interliners, so if wanting this option, work with medium-weight to heavy-weight fabrics.

### PRIVACY

Privacy is essential, especially in bedrooms and bathrooms. A breeze wafting through sheer curtains can add a touch of romance to any room; however the vibe can be intrusive if you're overlooked. During the day, sheers diffuse light, but at night light from inside is projected out, effectively turning your room into a TV for the neighbors. Similarly, large folding doors opening onto a garden or balcony look fantastic during the day, but being faced with your reflection at night can be a touch eerie. Think carefully about how to dress these types of windows. They're often made to take advantage of the whole wall space, which doesn't leave you with much room for poles, tracks, or fabric stack. Heavy curtains may not fit so well with this type of window design, so try attaching poles to the ceiling and hanging simple curtain panels instead, which can enhance a modern look and feel.

### DARKNESS

It's probably fair to say that most people need complete darkness to sleep well. Blocking out light is paramount, whether it's sunlight or a streetlight you're contending with. Make sure your treatment covers the window completely. Use blinds with a blackout backing, but don't fit within the window recess, as light will pour in on all sides. A combination of blinds and curtains is also an option, allowing for more choice with color and pattern.

To maximize light, make sure your curtains and blinds can be fully opened to expose the entire window. Curtain poles and tracks will need to sit beyond the edges of the window to account for curtain stacking space. Install blinds outside the window recess so that they can be fully opened.

### RADIATORS

Radiators can be a real pain. For optimum output, they're more often than not positioned directly under a window. Floor-length curtains will of course cover radiators when closed, keeping your windows nice and toasty but not the room! Instead, consider making sill-length curtains.

**Opposite:** Gap Interiors/Colin Poole

# Function and Form continued

## FORM

### MOOD

What room are we in and what mood or atmosphere are we trying to create? As well as color and pattern, fabric type and treatment can dictate mood. Velvets, damasks, and silks are more formal, whereas chintz and linen feel casual. The choice of curtain headings is also important. Simple pencil pleats create even folds and are easy on the eye. More formal treatments, such as box or pinch pleats, work especially well on floor-length curtains in a grand setting, but they can look overly fussy when used on sill-length curtains in a new build. With some of the fancy headings, be sure to use a more rigid fabric to aid the hang. The neat, uniform waves of an eyelet curtain give a stylish and modern vibe. Tab tops work well for lightweight fabrics, and can also have quite a casual feel.

### SETTING

There are so many window styles, it's hard to cover them all. When selecting poles, tracks, and blinds, consider the room as a whole. Where there are multiple windows, hang all the poles and blinds at the same height. Two identical windows that sit side by side can be treated as one window if they're close together, and you can use one half of a pair of curtains for each. If treated separately, keep them identical. Large French windows need a lot of curtain and therefore a lot of stacking space, so extend the pole beyond the outer edges of the doors. Bay windows need poles or tracks that are designed to move around corners—use these in conjunction with passing rings so that the curtain glides over the brackets. Add a little extra to the fabric width and return the outer edge of the curtain to the wall. Feed the last curtain hook through a screw eye in the wall. Individual blinds for each section of the bay can also work well.

Large folding doors often leave little room for tracks, poles, and stacking space, so consider attaching poles to the ceiling and using simple modern curtain panels. If valances are your thing, be sure that they are in proportion to the rest of the room.

A bathroom needs privacy, and the finished window treatment needs to withstand moisture. It's best to avoid folds in fabric, as they will play host to mold and mildew. Simple, washable blinds work well. Window film underneath a blind is also an option, as it provides privacy and is easy to attach and clean. Kitchens are also wet areas. In this case, there's more than just moisture to contend with—there's the added bonus of grease and smell. Again, blinds that are easy to remove and are able to withstand cleaning are ideal.

### ASPECT

Are your windows north or south facing? How much light enters the room? Heavy window treatments involving multiple blinds and curtains will make a dark room darker. In a bright room, think about the colorfastness of the fabric. Bright colors such as pinks, greens, and blues are more susceptible to fading. Fabrics such as silks will deteriorate quickly when exposed to direct sunlight, so take this into consideration when making a decision about fabric.

**Opposite:** Gap Interiors/Mark Bolton

# CHAPTER 3

## Measuring and Planning

# Overview

It might sound pretty dull, but planning ahead and taking accurate measurements will make your life much easier. The hanging method for your curtains or blinds needs to be in place before measurements can be taken. Establish the makeup of your wall, select the correct fixings, and bring out the drill. Lined curtains can be pretty heavy—do you have enough brackets? Once in place, you can work out how many yards of fabric and lining you will need, as you don't want to overspend or under-buy. If required, remember to take into account any pattern matching. When it comes to cutting and stitching, clear a decent amount of space, and make sure you have a flat surface for measuring and marking. It's best to try and keep children and pets away, but an evening sewing in front of the TV with the family can be pretty relaxing!

**Opposite:** Photograph by Sherry Heck

# Tutorial
# Attaching a Curtain Pole to the Wall

Once you've decided on your window treatment, you'll need to get to grips with how to fix the pole or track to the wall. Even if you've never fancied yourself as a DIYer, this tutorial is pretty straightforward. Don't be daunted by the power tools!

## YOU WILL NEED - WALL TYPE A

- Curtain pole and brackets
- Electric hammer drill or SDS drill (the hammer action is for masonry)
- Spirit level
- Wall plugs
- Screws (see wall plugs for correct size)
- Masonry drill bit (see wall plugs for correct size)
- Hammer
- Pencil

## YOU WILL NEED - WALL TYPE B

- As above, plus helical wall plugs (which are self-drilling)

The first step is to work out what type of wall you have. There are primarily two types of walls:

**A** Brick or block covered in plaster.
**B** Drywall fixed to a wood or metal frame.

## ATTACHING FOR WALL TYPE A

To start, take two measurements—the height of the pole and the positioning of the brackets. To measure the pole height, ask someone to hold the pole horizontally in place for you, and then measure from the top of the window frame to the top of the pole. Make a light mark on the wall—you'll need this measurement for step 3. For the bracket measurement, lay the curtain pole on the floor with the brackets and finials in place. Measure the distance between the center of both brackets. Divide this measurement by two—you will need this measurement for step 4.

## ATTACHING FOR WALL TYPE B

For plasterboard walls, follow all the steps until step 8. At this point, use a self-drilling helical plasterboard fixing rather than drilling holes, and continue.

## STEPS FOR WALL TYPES A AND B

**1.** Find the center of the window and lightly mark with pencil on the wall or window frame.

**2.** Line up a spirit level with this mark and make a vertical line on the wall roughly where the pole will sit.

**3.** Mark the distance between the top of the window and the pole from the center line in step 1. Make a horizontal mark through the vertical one. You should now have a cross on the wall. This cross represents the center of the pole vertically and horizontally.

**4.** From this point mark the bracket measurement. Repeat on the opposite side of the center marks.

**5.** Horizontally line up a long spirit level on the center cross and out toward the bracket measurement. Mark a horizontal line. You will now have a cross, which is the center of your bracket. Repeat on the opposite side of the center marks.

**6.** Align the brackets appropriately, on the center of the cross, and mark the screw holes.

**7.** Gently hammer a screw into the center of the marks, just enough to make a small indent. This will prevent the drill from slipping in the next step.

**8.** Drill the holes. You can fold a sticky note in half and stick to the wall directly under the drilling point to catch any debris.

**9.** Insert the wall plugs and screw the brackets in place.

## IMPORTANT HEALTH AND SAFETY

Before drilling into any wall, make sure there are no electrics or plumbing in the drilling area.

---

**TIP**

If you only have a small spirit level, use in conjunction with a long piece of straight wood.

Wrap a piece of masking tape around the drill bit to limit the depth of the hole you are making.

---

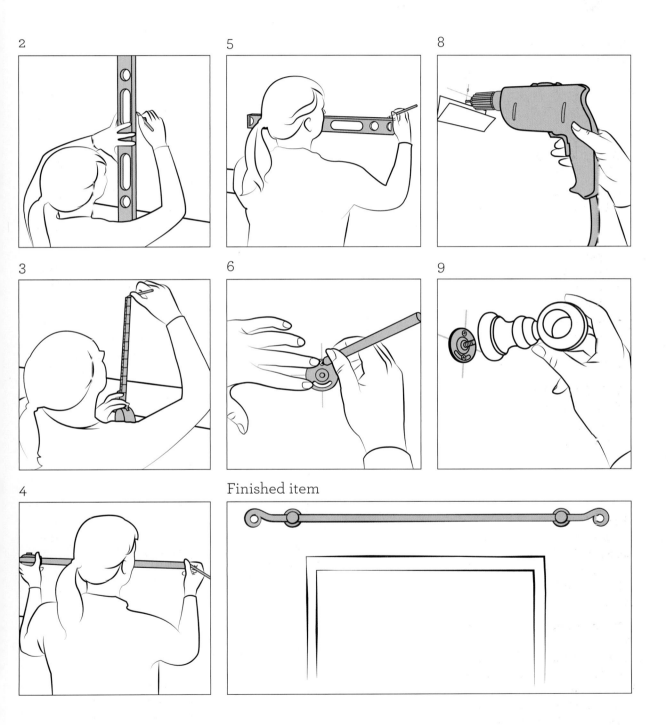

2

5

8

3

6

9

4

Finished item

# How to Measure for Curtains

If you don't already have your pole in situ, there are a few things you need to consider before buying your curtain fabric. To begin, you should measure the width of the window. To this measurement you'll need to add stacking space for the curtain on either side of the window. How much space you need depends on the weight of the fabric and what sort of tape gather will be used. Heavy lined velvet curtains will require a large amount of stacking space, while silk won't need as much.

Decide where you want your curtains to stop—at the sill or to the floor. If you want them to stop at the sill, it's best to make them a touch shorter so that they hang and hold their shape rather than drag—around ⅝in (1.5cm) is a good amount. It's also possible that a heavier fabric may drop over time, so take this into consideration. If you want the curtains to stop just below the sill, make them approximately 4in (10cm) longer so that the choice of length looks deliberate. Again, with the floor measurement it's best to stop short of the floor so they hang well. For a puddled look, add another 4–6in (10–15cm).

Use the diagram on the right as a guide to measuring for curtains. Always measure using a steel measuring tape rather than a fabric one, as these have a tendency to stretch over time, and get up on a stepladder to make it easier for yourself. Take written notes of the measurements, and measure twice to double-check. Here's how to take the measurements:

**1.** With the pole in place, measure the width of pole or track, excluding the finials.

**2.** Measure from the drop point to your chosen curtain length (i.e., sill or floor). The drop point will be either the curtain ring eyelet if you are using header tape and hooks, or the top of the pole for tab, tie top and eyelet curtains.

**3.** The heading height is the distance between the curtain ring eye and just below the pole. Traditionally, the upper part of the curtain ring should be visible above the curtain, but I quite like hiding the rings and pole completely. It's all down to personal taste. Having established the overall length and width of your finished curtains, it's time to work out how much fabric you will need (see page 46).

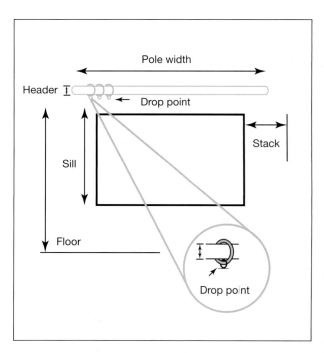

**Opposite:** Gap Interiors/Bill Kingston

# Calculating Fabric

It might seem logical that each curtain is half the width of the curtain pole, but this isn't the case! For even a simple pleated curtain you will need a surprising amount of fabric. The extra fabric required is referred to as fullness, and varies depending on the different header tapes and styles you choose. Typically, curtains need two to two-and-a-half times the curtain pole width for fullness (see chart below). In this example, I'm using two and a half fullness.

## NUMBER OF FABRIC WIDTHS REQUIRED FOR 2–2½ TIMES FULLNESS CURTAINS

If math isn't your strong point, use the chart below for an indication of how much fabric you'll need.

| LENGTH RANGE OF POLE | NUMBER OF FABRIC WIDTHS REQUIRED (BASED ON 54IN/137CM-WIDE FABRIC) |
|---|---|
| 48–63in (120–160cm) | 3 |
| 60–90in (150–230cm) | 4 |
| 86–118in (220–300cm) | 5 |
| 110–141in (280–360cm) | 6 |
| 130–169in (330–430cm) | 7 |
| 154–197in (390–500cm) | 8 |

## MEASURING FULLNESS

**1.** Measure the length of your curtain pole excluding finials Pole length = 70in (180cm).

**2.** Multiply 70in (180cm) by 2.5 (fullness) = 175in (450cm).

**3.** Add 8in (20cm) for ease and overlap (overlap refers to the center of the window) = 183in (470cm).

**4.** Add side hem allowance. In this case I'm allowing for four 4in (10cm) side hems = 199in (510cm).

**5.** Divide this by the width of your chosen fabric (i.e., the width of the fabric bolt—mine is 54in/137cm) = 3.68 (3.72).

Round up to the nearest full or half width—in this case, four fabric widths are needed for the two curtain panels.

## MEASURING LENGTH

With your pole and rings in place, measure from your drop point (eyes on the rings) to the chosen finished length of your curtains. In this case, my drop point is 102in (260cm).

**1.** Add your hem and header allowances, in this case 8in (20cm) and 8in (20cm).
102in (260cm) + 8in (20cm) + 8in (20cm) = 118in (300cm).

**2.** Multiply by four widths of fabric.
118in (300cm) x 4 = 472in (1,200cm)

## NOTE

If using patterned fabric you will need more fabric to account for pattern matching. See pages 48–50 for more about pattern matching.

**Opposite:** Gap Interiors/Mark Scott

# Pattern Matching

Once you've made your pattern choice, measured your windows, calculated your fabric, and decided on the headings and other details, the chances are you'll need to do a bit of pattern matching. Before you get down to stitching, however, there are some more decisions and calculating to do.

### STYLE

You'll first need to decide how you want your pattern to sit. Some patterns are balanced, and others have areas where the pattern is bolder or stronger in color. Visually, it's better to keep the heavier part of the design toward the bottom of the curtain. This will stop the curtain looking top-heavy, and your eye will be drawn to the falling drape of the curtain. Try folding the fabric at different points and hanging it over the pole or in a way that you can see the design. It's important to get this right.

It may be that your curtain only needs one and a half widths of fabric. If this is the case, keep the halves to the outer edges of your curtains. Your curtains will look more balanced with two full widths meeting in the center when drawn.

### PATTERN REPEATS

You have your basic curtain measurements and you've made your pattern choice. Those measurements now need to be jigged a little to accommodate the fabric's repeating pattern. You can find this information within the fabric details, or on the fabric bolt. You can also check the repeat yourself. To do this, choose a strong point in the design near the selvage, then measure down the length of fabric until you reach the same point. Do the same across the width. These measurements are the pattern repeat.

## One-and-a-half width curtains

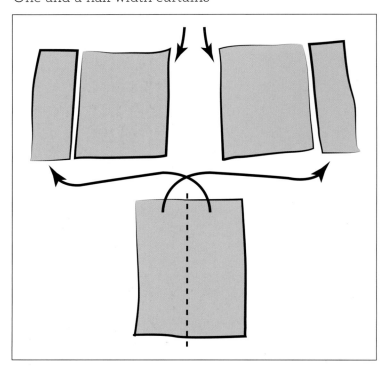

## CALCULATING

Calculate the curtain measurements by adding the pattern repeat measurement to the drop measurement (this is your curtain including the hem and heading allowance). Let's say your drop measurement is 70in (178cm) and the pattern repeat is 15in (38cm)—you will need 85in (216cm) for every drop.

## CHECK BEFORE CUTTING

It's easy to assume that your fabric pattern lies straight on the bolt, but it's good practice to check that everything is straight before cutting. If the pattern is bold, your eye could be drawn to small shifts in the pattern, especially when the curtains are drawn. If your printed pattern is off-kilter you'll need to cut according to the pattern and not to the grain. This process can feel unnatural, but it will be worth it.

## CUTTING HALF-DROP REPEATS

As with all curtain projects, make yourself some space and iron the fabric flat, then follow these steps.

**1.** Decide how you are going to position the pattern on the curtain. Cut your first panel to the finished drop size—this is the curtain length plus the header and hem.

**2.** With your panel lying flat, unroll another length of fabric next to it. You'll need to move the fabric up a little to match the pattern, leaving you with extra fabric above and below your first panel. Using your first panel as a guide, mark across the top and bottom of the second panel using chalk. Double-check the pattern match and then cut the fabric. Continue this process until you have all the desired panels.

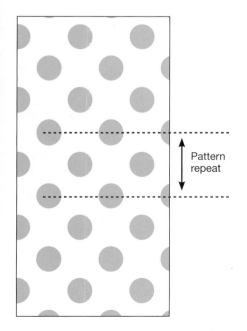

Pattern repeat

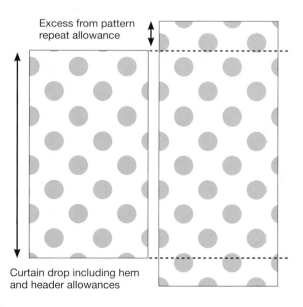

Excess from pattern repeat allowance

Curtain drop including hem and header allowances

# Tutorial
# Pattern Matching continued

## STITCHING THE DROPS TOGETHER

**1.** Trim off the selvage from one of your curtain drops. Turn over the edge so that the wrong sides are together. Press this fold flat.

**2.** Lay this over the second curtain drop, right sides facing, and match the pattern along the fold.

**3.** Fold down the top flap and pin along the creased (pressed) line. Machine stitch along the crease and press open the seam. You can also hand tack the crease line first and check the pattern match from the right side. It's good to do this if the fabric is difficult to handle.

---

**TIP**

Machine stitch from the hem to the top of the curtains. Of course, it's unlikely you will go out of alignment, but if you do then the mistake will be lost in the folds at the top of the curtain!

If you are using striped fabric, join the widths within the stripe itself. Trying to match down the edge of a stripe is pretty tricky, and your eye will be drawn to any mistakes.

---

1

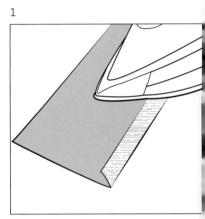

2

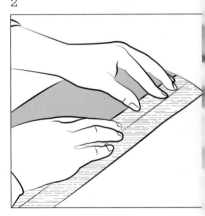

3

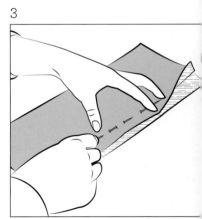

**Opposite:** Gap Interiors/Douglas Gibb

# CHAPTER 4

## Sewing Basics

# Overview

If you've never handled a sewing machine or threaded a needle, don't fear. The skills needed to complete the tutorials in this chapter are fairly simple. When buying a sewing machine, seek advice from sewing friends or your local sewing store. Most basic machines have the features required for curtain making, so you don't need to buy the most expensive model. For the best stitching results, take the time to select the correct needles and check the tension each time you switch fabrics. A little patience goes a long way. As far as hand stitching goes, you won't need any fancy embroidery skills, but it's useful to have a few basic stitches under your belt.

**Opposite:** Gap Interiors/Bieke Claessens; Designer: Nico Vink

# Sewing Machines

Everyone should own a sewing machine. Yours doesn't need to be expensive or overly sophisticated to make curtains or complete the tutorials in this book. If you're on the hunt for a machine, the choice can be daunting. You can spend hours wading through websites looking for the best deal, but my advice is to visit your local fabric or department store and talk to those in the know. Perhaps your local fabric or craft store offers courses—having someone sit with you and talk you through the basics is invaluable. Remember, always look after your machine and regularly clean and maintain it.

## NEEDLES

A blunt needle can result in missed stitches, broken thread, and holes in your fabric. It's good practice to replace the needle for every 4–6 hours of sewing. Clunking or popping noises from your machine really aren't good, and this could be a sign your needle needs changing. Every machine will come with instructions. If you don't have them in printed form, it's likely you'll find them online. Check the troubleshooting pages if anything looks or sounds strange. When replacing a needle, make sure the new one is fully inserted into the machine.

As well as replacing needles regularly, you'll need to think about the fabric you are using. Different weights of fabric require different needle sizes. Here's a basic overview of needle sizes and fabric weights:

**Sizes 9–11:** Lightweight voiles
**Sizes 12–14:** Medium-weight fabrics
**Sizes 16—18:** Heavyweight fabrics

## SHANK

Commonly, needles for domestic sewing machines have a flat shank, whereas shanks for industrial machines are generally round. For domestic machines, the flat side of the needle faces to the left as you look at the machine. Always check the instructions for your machine.

## GROOVE

The groove helps guide the thread toward the eye of the needle.

## SCARF

The scarf is the cutaway above the eye of the needle. This allows the bobbin hook to grab the thread under the throat plate to create a stitch.

## EYE

Thread passes through the eye of a needle. The size of the eye required depends on the size of thread.

## POINT AND TIP

As with the eye, the size, shape, and length of the point and tip varies from needle to needle.

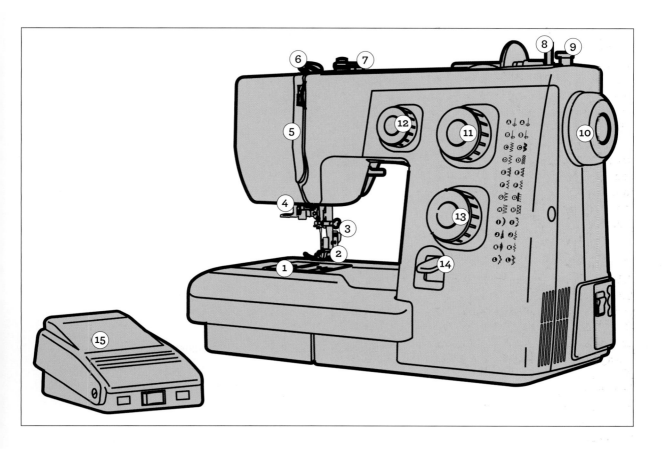

This is a basic sewing machine. Most machines will have the following elements built in:

1. Stitch plate
2. Presser foot
3. Needle clamp
4. Thread regulator
5. Thread take-up lever
6. Pre-tension stud
7. Thread tension adjustment knob
8. Thread holder pins
9. Bobbin spindle
10. Hand wheel
11. Stitch width knob
12. Needle position knob
13. Stitch length knob
14. Reverse stitch lever
15. Sewing machine foot pedal

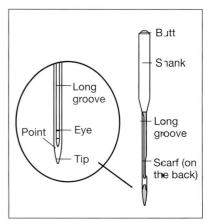

# Sewing Machines continued

## FEET

It's good to have a few different feet for your machine, but the straight stitch foot is generally all that's needed for making curtains.

### 1. STRAIGHT STITCH FOOT

Ideal for most normal stitching. The wide sole is great for stitching light and heavyweight fabrics, as it prevents the fabric from puckering.

### 2. WALKING FOOT

A walking foot can come in handy, as both the top and bottom fabric move at the same pace, meaning that it's less likely your fabric will slip. This is especially useful when pattern matching, and is also good when using thicker fabrics.

### 3. ZIPPER FOOT

As the name suggests, this foot is good for sewing zippers. It's also a good stand-in for a piping foot if you don't have one. A zipper foot is thin and enables you to get close to the zipper or piping. It's unlikely you'll need to add a zipper or piping to your curtain, but it's always handy to have one in your sewing kit.

### 4. BLIND HEM FOOT

This foot is ideal for sewing blind hems. The only visible element on the right side of your fabric will be a tiny ladder stitch. The foot has a metal strip that butts up to the folded hem. The stitch will be straight, with the occasional zigzag into the curtain.

## THREAD

Poor-quality thread can cause crooked and looped stitches, puckered seams, frayed thread, and needle breakage. A good-quality cotton or polyester-coated cotton thread is a good choice for most projects. Use silk threads on delicate fabrics. When starting your project, make sure you are using the correct thread and needle size with the correct tension. And remember, the higher the thread count number, the thinner the thread.

### TOP SPOOL THREAD

Incorrect threading is one of the most common causes of incorrect stitching. Check your machine's instructions before attempting to thread. Commonly, you always thread the needle from front to back. When you get to this stage, continue to pull the thread through by about 6in (15cm).

### THREADING THE BOBBIN

**1.** Place the empty bobbin on the bobbin spool and your reel of thread on the thread holder pin, with the thread coming out from behind the reel.

**2.** Take the thread from the reel and pass it clockwise around the pre-tension stud and to the empty bobbin. Wind the thread around the bobbin a few times in a clockwise direction.

**3.** Make sure your machine is set to wind a bobbin (check your instructions). Many will disengage from the stitching mechanism so the needle no longer moves up and down. Press the foot control to start the machine. When the bobbin is full, the machine should stop automatically.

1

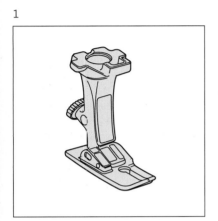

4

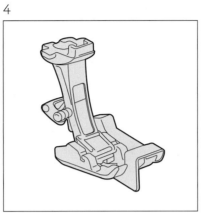

**TIP**
When choosing thread, if there's not a perfect color match for your fabric, it's generally best to go for a darker shade.

2

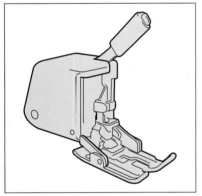

## Threading the bobbin

3

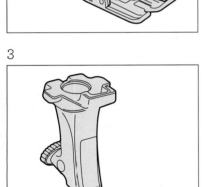

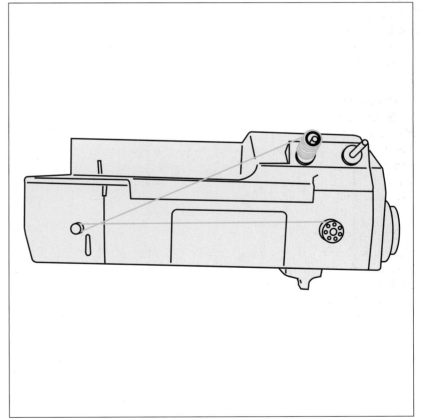

# Sewing Machines continued

## INSERTING THE BOBBIN INTO THE CASE

**1.** Hold the bobbin case in one hand and insert the bobbin with the thread running clockwise.

**2.** Continue to pull the thread clockwise and move it into the slot.

**3.** Pull under the spring and into the open area. The bobbin should turn clockwise when you pull the thread.

**4.** Hold the latch open on the opposite side of the bobbin case. Insert the bobbin into the machine with the finger facing upward (this may be different depending on your machine).

**5.** Now bring the thread up from the bobbin. Pull roughly 6in (15cm) of thread through the needle and hold it in your left hand. Close the bobbin casing and turn the hand wheel toward you to lower the needle. The needle will catch the bobbin thread and pull it up and through. Continue turning the hand wheel until the take-up lever is fully raised. Pull the upper thread. As you do this, the bobbin thread will be brought up through the stitch plate. Take both threads through the slot in the presser foot and bring to the side.

## TENSION

The tension of the bobbin and the top spool thread need to be balanced in order for the machine to stitch correctly. Usually, the tension is changed in the top spool, but check your machine's instructions. You may need to alter the tension on the bobbin, but this is generally a last resort. Check the tension using some scrap fabric. As a rule, you should use the fabric you are about to stitch, and in as many layers as in your project.

## 6. PERFECT TENSION

If the line of stitching looks the same on both sides of your fabric, then the tension is perfect. The bobbin thread and the top spool thread interlock in the center of your fabric.

## 7. TOP SPOOL THREAD LOOSE

If the top thread is showing on the underside of the fabric, then your top spool tension is loose. Turn the tension wheel one notch higher and stitch again.

## 8. TOP SPOOL THREAD TIGHT

If the thread from the bobbin side is showing on the top side of the fabric, then the top spool is too tight. Turn the tension wheel one notch lower and stitch again.

## GETTING READY TO SEW

Get comfortable. Position the machine so that you are in line with the needle. Don't strain yourself. Once you get going it can be difficult to tear yourself away, but with a bad sitting position you may not be able to keep going. Feed the fabric through smoothly—don't push or hold it back. When you finish stitching, make sure the needle is in the raised position (some machines automatically bring the needle up). Take the work away from the machine at the rear. Snip the threads with about 6in (15cm) left loose.

1

4

6

2

5

7

3

8

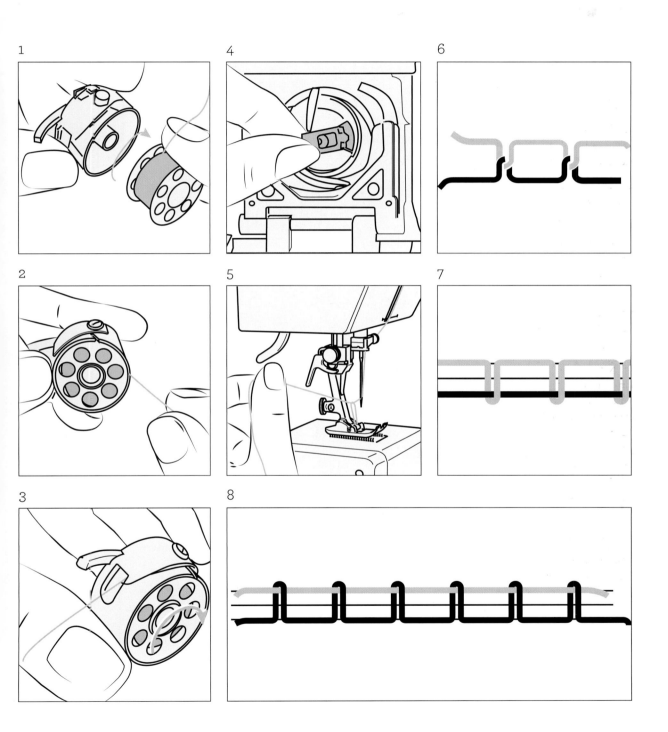

# Basic Stitches

Even if you're a devout machinist, having a few hand stitches under your belt is never a bad thing. In traditional curtain making, the majority of the stitching is made by hand. I often find it strangely therapeutic—slowing down the process and restoring some calm is surely good for the soul. Here are some useful stitches for making curtains and for other soft furnishing projects. I've come across many variations; if you have a preferred method, feel free to stick to what you know.

## 1. SLIP STITCH

There are variations to this stitch in dressmaking, but this is the method I use for curtains and upholstery. The stitch needs to sit in the fold of at least one of the fabrics for it to work. First, make a stitch into the fold of fabric, then make the next stitch directly into the other piece of fabric, and repeat. The stitch should not be visible when completed.

## 2. STAB STITCH

A lovely little stitch that quickly holds together layers of fabric but is barely visible—if you use matching thread, that is. To create the stitch, make three or four small stitches directly on top of each other through all layers of fabric. I use this stitch in the Roman Blinds (see pages 110–115) and Roll-up Blinds (see pages 106–109) tutorials.

## 3. BUTTONHOLE STITCH

As the name suggests, this stitch is commonly used for finishing buttonholes. I use this stitch to secure the blind rings in the Roman Blinds tutorial (see pages 110–115). Pass the needle through the fabric, under the top of the ring. Wrap the thread around the needle and continue to pull through the ring, and repeat. The ring will be wrapped in thread that sits side by side.

## 4. HERRINGBONE STITCH

Apart from being visually satisfying, the herringbone stitch is good for securing side hems to linings. The stitch should not be visible from the right side of the curtain. Try not to pull the stitch too tight, as it will pucker the fabric.

With the curtain right-side down, secure a length of thread in the folded edge of the hem. Move the needle diagonally up and to the right. Make a small stitch into the lining, just above the folded hem. Move the needle diagonally down and to the right and make a small stitch into the folded hem.

## 5–6. BLIND HEM STITCH

As the name suggests, the blind hem stitch is barely visible from the right side of the fabric, but if you look closely you'll see a tiny stitch. It is similar in structure to the herringbone stitch, but without the crossing threads. Turn back the hem and make your first stitch through the layers on the reverse of the curtain. Move to the right if you're right-handed and to the left if you're left-handed. Make a tiny stitch through the main fabric, then move along and make another stitch through the hem fabric, and so on.

## 7. SERGE STITCH

This is long stitch, perfect for securing side hems to interlining. In this case, the stitch will not go through to the right side of the curtain. I use this stitch in the Roman Blinds tutorial (see pages 110–115). With the curtain panel right-side down, secure a length of thread through the folded hem and interlining. Bring the needle down no more than 2in (5cm) at a slight diagonal. Make a small horizontal stitch through the fabric and interlining, close to the inside edge of the hem.

## 8. LOCK STITCH

Each stitch is locked in place as you go. You can use it to secure fabric to lining or interlining so that the layers don't billow out. The stitches should be a handspan apart and fairly loose. Begin by securing a length of thread through the fabric, lining and interlining, if using. Move the needle to the left—use your hand as a measuring guide—and pass through the lining and interlining. Before pulling completely through, make a knot in the thread.

1 Slip stitch

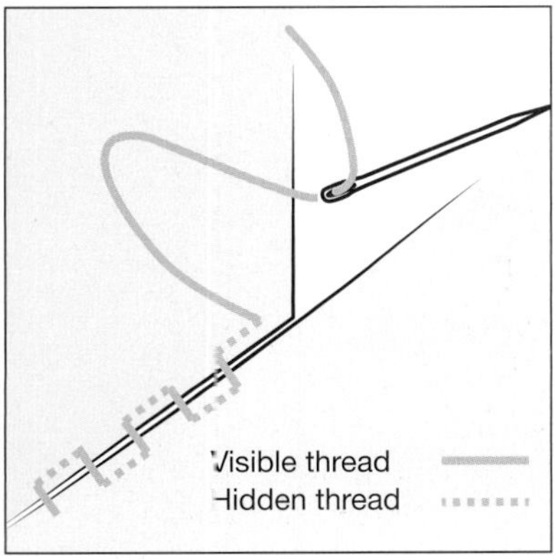

Visible thread
Hidden thread

4 Herringbone stitch

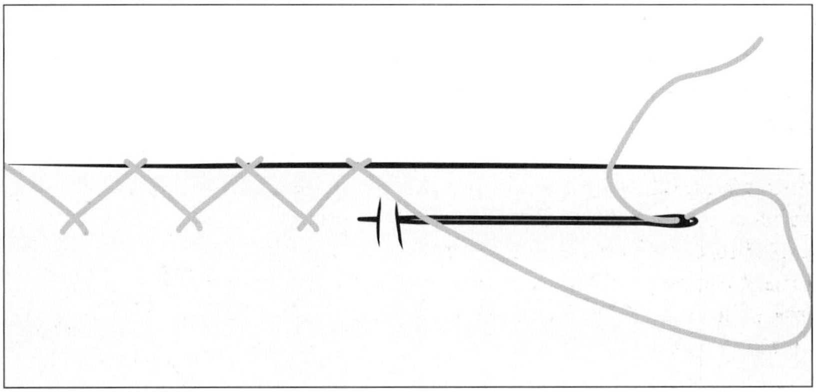

2 Stab stitch

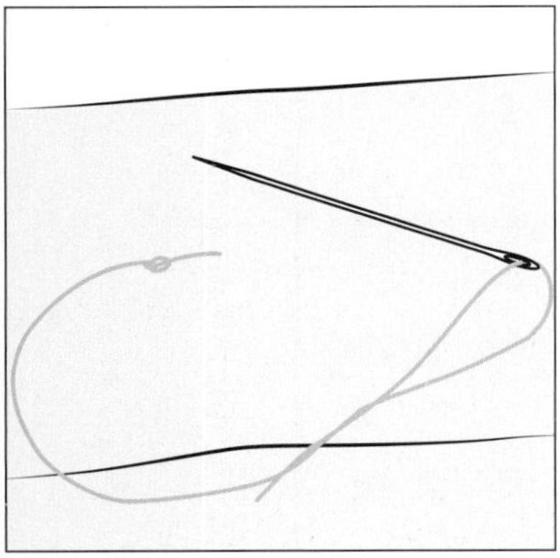

5 Blind hem stitch

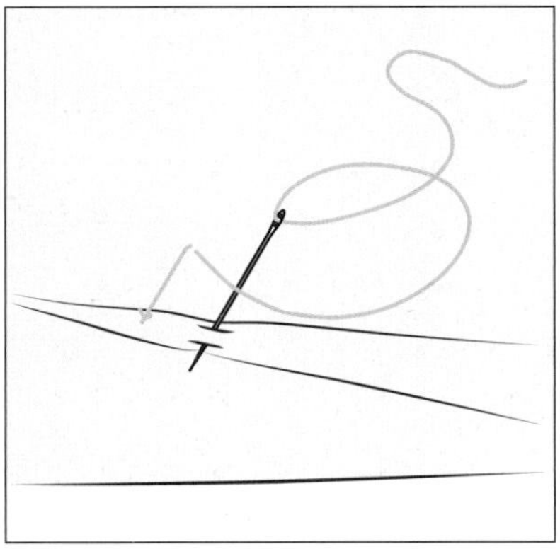

7 Serge stitch

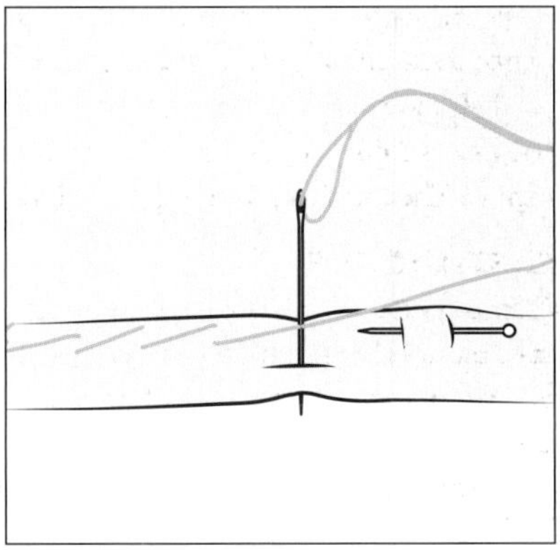

3 Buttonhole stitch

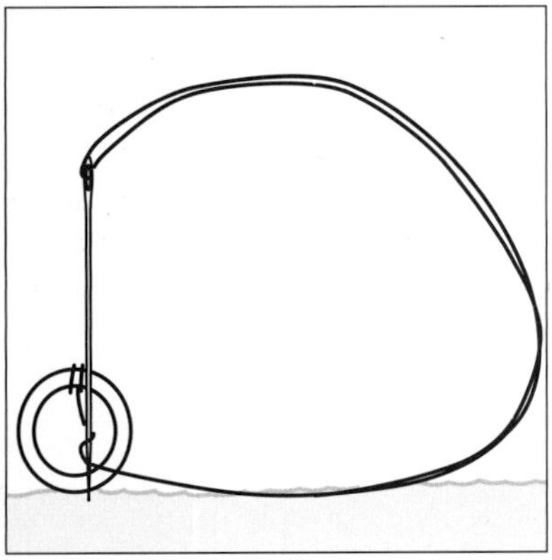

6 Blind hem stitch

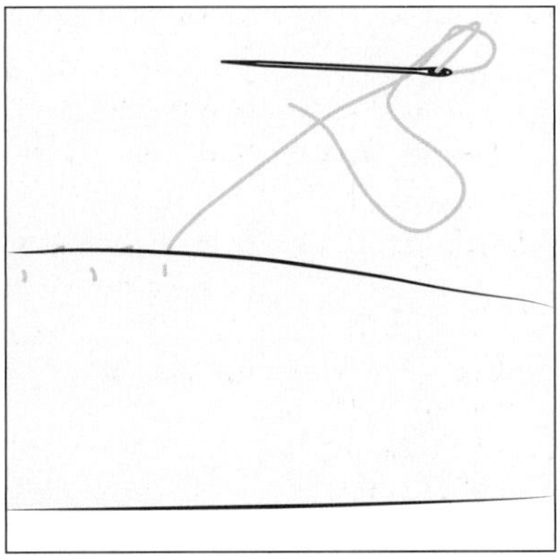

8 Lock stitch

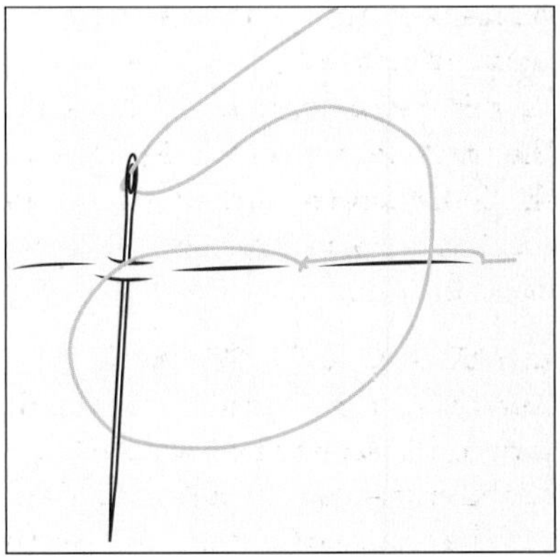

# How to Sew a Seam

## BASIC SEAMS AND SEWING TECHNIQUES

Many sewing machines are set up to perform several fancy stitches, but with most soft furnishing projects you'll only need to use the straight or zigzag setting. Based on the type of fabric you're working with, any adjustments you make will likely be to do with stitch length and tension.

### STRAIGHT STITCH

The most common machine stitch is as simple as it sounds. It's used in most soft furnishing projects.

### TOPSTITCH

A straight stitch that's used as decoration, to hold hems in place, and for added strength. Generally, you would use a slightly thicker thread for the topstitch. Think about using a contrasting thread as a statement feature! Always test the stitch on a scrap piece of fabric before you begin.

### ZIGZAG STITCH

The zigzag stitch is used to cover the raw edges of fabric and prevent fraying. If you're not lucky enough to own or have access to a serger, then this is the stitch for you. Fabric widths are joined using a straight stitch, and the open edges can then be finished off with the zigzag. I use a zigzag stitch in the Ruffles tutorial (see pages 128–129).

### SEAMS

Following are some of the most common seams for curtain making. Try to get into the habit of pressing every seam you make. It might sound tedious, but you'll have more control over the finished piece if you do. I pretty much always use a ⅝in (1.5cm) seam allowance as my default. You may have your preferred size, so stick to what you know.

### PLAIN SEAM

**1.** Place two pieces of fabric right sides together and pin. Sewing machines have a seam allowance marker next to the needle. If you are using your own measurement, then mark your stitch line with some tailor's chalk.

**2.** Hold the thread from the bobbin and the needle behind the foot. Sew a few stitches forward along the line, stop, and reverse-stitch over the first stitches, then continue forward. This will secure your seam. Repeat the backstitch when you come to the end.

**3.** Remove from the machine and snip the threads close to the fabric. Finish by pressing the seam with an iron, right sides together. Follow by ironing with the seam opened out if you are making a flat seam.

**4.** Neaten the edges with a zigzag stitch.

### FRENCH SEAM

The French seam holds the raw edges of fabric neatly inside the finished seam. I use this technique in Working with Sheer Fabrics (see pages 80–81). This type of seam is not really suitable for bulky fabrics.

**1.** Place the fabric with the wrong sides facing and machine stitch ¼in (6mm) from the raw edge. Press the seam open.

**2.** Turn the fabric so that the right sides are facing. Machine stitch ⅜in (1cm) from the seamed edge to enclose the raw edges.

### FLAT FELL SEAM

Flat fell seams lie flat and are strong, so they're good for joining widths of unlined curtains together.

**1.** Place the fabric right sides together. Machine stitch with a ⅝in (1.5cm) seam allowance and press.

**2.** Trim one side of the seam by about half.

**3.** Turn the longer seam over and under the trimmed edge. Press again and straight-stitch together, sewing close to the folded edge.

### CURVED SEAMS

When stitching a curved seam you'll need to clip or notch the seam allowance to help ease the fabric into shape—notch for outer curved edges and clip for inner curves. Make sure you cut straight toward the seam and not on the angle. I use notches in the Soft Valance tutorial (see pages 138–139).

## Straight stitch

## French seam

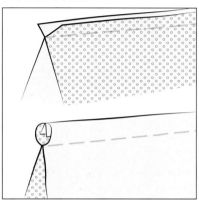

## Flat fell seam

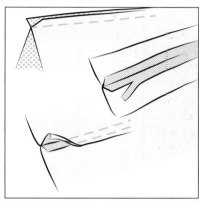

## Zigzag stitch

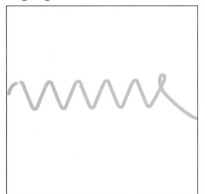

## Curved seam

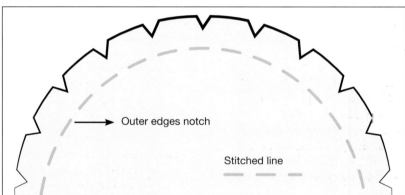

Outer edges notch

Stitched line

## Plain seam

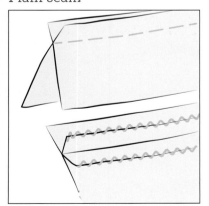

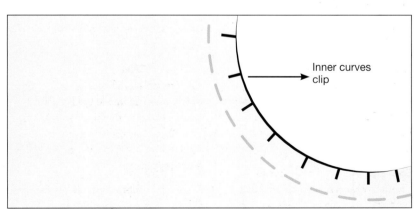

Inner curves clip

# Troubleshooting

## GENERAL SEWING MACHINE CARE

- Clean your machine regularly. Fabric and thread both produce lint, which can work its way into all areas. Your machine probably came with a small brush—use it to clean all areas and under the bobbin case. Use an air blower or compressed air to get into any harder to reach areas.
- More often than not, most problems with stitching result from incorrect threading. Always check this first before fiddling with tension dials.
- When threading, make sure the presser foot is in the up position. If the foot is down it will mean the thread will not slip fully between the tension discs.
- Make sure the bobbin is facing the correct way in the bobbin case.
- Remove any thread on the bobbin before winding a new thread. This will make sure the new thread is evenly wound and at the proper tension.
- Wind the bobbin at a slow or medium speed.
- Check that you are using the correct stitch size for the fabric you are sewing.
- Make sure you use the correct needles and bobbins. Incorrect use can cause damage to your machine.
- Use the same weight thread in the top and in the bobbin, and make sure it's good quality.
- Always test the stitch on a scrap piece of fabric before starting the job at hand.

## THREAD IS BUNCHING ON THE REVERSE OF THE FABRIC

- Make sure you're using good-quality thread. Don't buy from the bargain bin.
- Keep hold of the top and bottom threads when you start stitching.
- Make sure your presser foot is in the down position.
- Check the tension of the top thread.

## THREAD BUNCHING ON TOP OF THE FABRIC

- Check that your bobbin is inserted and threaded correctly.

## BREAKING NEEDLE

- Check that the needle is the correct size for your job.
- How many layers of fabric are you sewing through? Your needle may not be strong enough if you're trying to sew through many layers. If so, replace with a stronger needle.
- If you force the fabric through the machine, the needle can move and hit the stitch plate, causing it to break.
- Make sure the needle is in the correct position for the pressure foot you are using.

## BREAKING THREAD

- Start by checking the machine is correctly threaded.
- Make sure you are using a good-quality thread.
- Check the needle for burred edges. These can easily cut the thread.
- Check that the top thread doesn't have too much tension.

## BREAKING BOBBIN THREAD

- The bobbin could be incorrectly threaded.
- The edges of plastic bobbins can become damaged, causing the bobbin to wobble in the case, and changing the tension. This can also happen to a metal bobbin if it has been dropped.
- The stitch plate hole could possibly be damaged.

## UNEVEN OR SKIPPED STITCHES

- Check the size and type of needle. It may be incorrect for the job.
- The needle could be blunt, in which case you should change it. It's good practice to change the needle every 4–6 hours of sewing.
- Make sure the needle is inserted fully into the shaft. If not, the needle will be unable to pull up the bobbin thread.
- Make sure the thread is the same weight in the bobbin and on the top.
- If none of the above works, check the instructions for your machine. It could quite possibly be a timing issue.

### MACHINE DOES NOT FEED THE FABRIC

- The stitch length could be too short. Lengthen it and try stitching again.
- Lower the feed dogs.
- The feed dogs could be full of dust or dirt. Clean with the sewing machine brush.

### THE SEAM IS TOO LOOSE

- The thread tension is too loose. Try adjusting the tension.

### MACHINE WON'T PICK UP THE BOBBIN THREAD

- Make sure the bobbin is inserted correctly and the bobbin is the right way round in the bobbin case.
- Check the needle is inserted correctly.
- If none of the above works, check the instructions for your machine. It could quite possibly be a timing issue.

**Right:** Gap Interiors/Douglas Gibb

# SECTION 2

## Techniques

# CHAPTER 5

## Curtains and Drapes

# Overview

Curtains are so simple to make. From no-sew drapes to working with heading tapes and eyelets, the following tutorials can be completed in a weekend or even a day, and will totally transform a room. For successful curtain making, take your time, measuring twice—or perhaps three times— and sew as accurately as you can. Thankfully, you'll only need the most basic of sewing skills, as much of the machine work will be straight-line stitching. You'll need as much space as possible, so clear the tables or the floor and declare the zone child- and pet-free!

**Previous page:** Photograph by Sherry Heck
**Opposite:** Lara Cameron/Ink & Spindle

# Tutorial
# No-sew Drapes

This is a great solution for a lunchtime window makeover! If you don't have access to a sewing machine and you don't have the time or inclination to hand stitch, then these are the curtains for you. If you are unsure of your cutting skills you could even ask your local fabric store to cut the fabric for you.

## YOU WILL NEED

- Fabric
- Scissors or rotary cutter
- Fusible web
- Iron
- Damp cloth
- Drapery clip rings
- Curtain rod—already fixed

**1.** Measure your windows (see pages 44–45) and cut your fabric to size using scissors or a rotary cutter. Also take into account the width of the fusible web—if the fusible web is 1in (2.5cm), then add 2in (5cm) to each side of your fabric for turning in.

**2.** Turn up the fabric edges (wrong sides together) by 1in (2.5cm) and press. Continue this process around the whole curtain.

**3.** Measure and cut four pieces of fusible web for each edge. Place along one edge of the curtain. Turn the fabric up by another 1in (2.5cm), concealing the fusible web.

**4.** Check the heat of the iron on a scrap piece of fabric first. Bring the iron down on top of this fold and hold for about 10 seconds (check the instructions supplied with the fusible web). Continue bringing the iron down onto the fabric. Don't slide the iron, as this could move the fabric out of line. If necessary, use a damp cloth between the iron and curtain to prevent the fabric from burning.

**5.** Continue this process around all sides of the curtain. When you hit the corners, fold in to make a mitered corner, snipping away any excess fabric. Add more fusible web and press again.

**6.** Space your drapery clip rings about 4in (10cm) apart along the top of the curtain. Start and finish with one on either end. Clip to the fabric and hang your finished curtain on the curtain rod!

## MITERED CORNERS

A mitered corner is a perfect square corner with no visible raw edges. There are a couple of different techniques for mitering.

### A quick miter

Make your bottom hem folds. Make your side hem fold, turning the bottom edge under at a 45° angle from the corner. If the corner is too bulky you can cut away excess fabric from within the fold.

### A true miter

**1.** Position the curtain right side down, double-fold the bottom hem, followed by the side hems. Place a pin in the corner and fold back the hems by one fold.

**2.** Fold the corner into the curtain so that both edges are parallel to the side and bottom of the curtain.

**3.** Fold the side and bottom hems in. Where they meet will be a perfect 45° angle. Press.

2

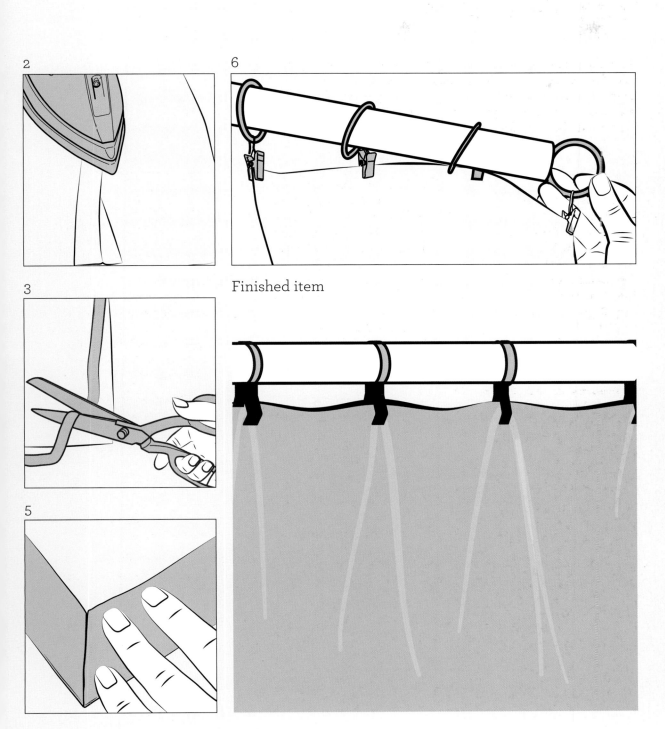

3

5

6

Finished item

# Tutorial
# Basic Unlined Curtains

These are the simplest sewn curtains of them all! Using this technique, your windows can be transformed in an afternoon. In this example I'll be machine stitching and finishing with a simple casement for the curtain pole, so there's no need for heading tape or eyelets. If you are new to making curtains, choose a fabric that is easy to work with—a medium-weight cotton is a good choice. If you feel your fabric is too light, you could add drapery weights at step 4. Before stitching the curtain together, fold the fabric over the curtain rod and see how it hangs.

## YOU WILL NEED

- Tape measure or yardstick
- Fabric
- Scissors
- Pins
- Iron
- Thread
- Sewing machine
- Curtain rod
- Drapery weights (optional)

**1.** Refer to the measurement diagram opposite. Begin by measuring your curtain drop and add 4in (10cm) for your hem and 4in (10cm) for your side turns. The size of the heading casement will depend on the diameter of your curtain pole. Wrap a scrap piece of the fabric you are using around the pole, take this measurement and add a further 1in (2.5cm) to allow the curtain to slide more easily. In this example I am adding 6⅝in (16.5cm)—⅝in (1.5cm) to turn in the raw edge and 6in (15cm) to cover the pole. Once you have your measurements, cut your fabric to size.

**2.** Lay the fabric facedown. Turn one side in by 1in (2.5cm) and press. Turn in a further 1in (2.5cm) and press again. This process is referred to as a "double hem," or "double side turning" in this instance. Pin the hem in place and then repeat this process on the opposite side.

**3.** Machine stitch down both sides with a ⅝in (1.5cm) seam allowance. There is no need to start and end with a reverse stitch, as the sides will be overstitched in the following steps.

**4.** Lay the fabric facedown and turn up a 2in (5cm) double hem at the bottom of the curtain. For a 2in (5cm) double hem you will use 4in (10cm) of fabric. Press and pin. If you are using a sheer or lightweight fabric you can choose to use drapery weights in the corners of your curtain (see pages 74–75).

**5.** Machine stitch along the top of the folded edge using a ⅝in (1.5cm) seam allowance. Fold in or snip any stray threads from the sides of the curtains before stitching. Start and finish with a reverse stitch to secure.

**6.** For the top of the curtain, fold under ⅝in (1.5cm) of fabric and press. Fold over a further 6in (15cm), press, and pin. Machine stitch close to the folded edge, again tucking in or snipping any loose threads.

**7.** Run the curtain rod through the casing and there you have it—a curtain!

### TIP

For the hems and side turnings, it's easier to fold in the full amount, press, then fold in half.

## Measurement diagram

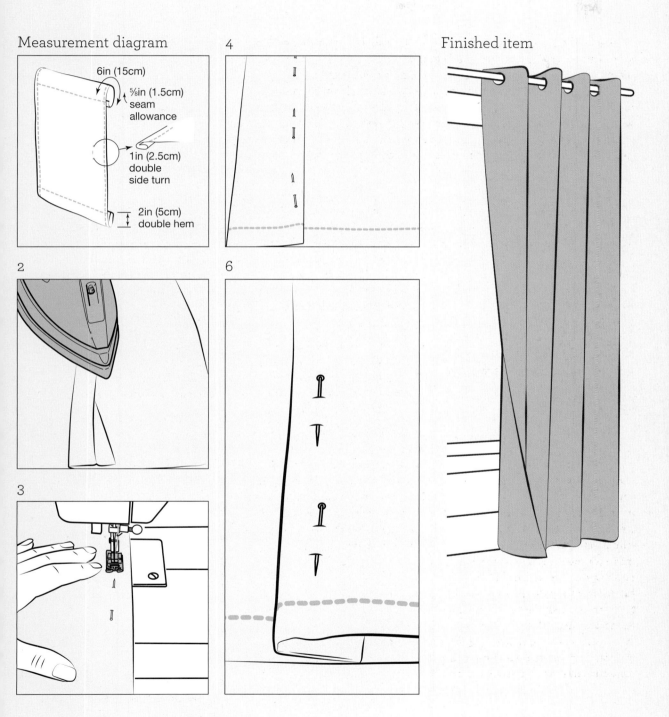

6in (15cm)

⅝in (1.5cm)
seam
allowance

1in (2.5cm)
double
side turn

2in (5cm)
double hem

4

2

6

3

## Finished item

# Tutorial
# Drapery Weights

If you find yourself raiding your parents' or grandparents' sewing kit, you may come across a naked lead weight. Although it's more common to find them in readymade pockets these days, you can still buy naked lead weights on their own. If you're a maker who likes to do everything from scratch, here's a simple guide for making weight pockets, or blister packs, if you prefer.

## YOU WILL NEED

- Lining fabric
- Drapery weights
- Ruler or tape measure
- Tailor's chalk
- Sewing machine
- Thread
- Scissors

**1.** Fold a piece of lining in half and machine stitch down one of the short sides.

**2.** Measure the weight, and add another quarter of its diameter. For standard lead weights, the total measurement works out to be about 1½in (4cm). Mark this measurement from the first stitched line and machine stitch a parallel line.

**3.** Machine another row of stitches parallel to this line, but about ¼in (6mm) along. Machine again at 1½in (4cm) then ¼in (6mm). Repeat along the width of the fabric.

**4.** Drop a weight into each channel and machine across the top to hold them in place. Machine again at ¼in (6mm) to form squares. Repeat this process until the pockets are full.

**5.** Cut between the weights in the ¼in (6mm) gap and use as needed.

## USING DRAPERY WEIGHTS

You can use drapery weights on unlined curtain panels to achieve a better drape. To do so, hand sew drapery weights onto the folded hem of your curtain (as per the finished illustration opposite). They should sit about ⅜in (1cm) from the bottom and sides. If your finished curtain has joined lengths of fabric to make up your widths, sew a weight at the base of each join, again at ⅜in (1cm) from the bottom of the curtain.

> **TIP**
> If you can't find drapery weights, try using small coins or washers instead—they can work just as well!

1

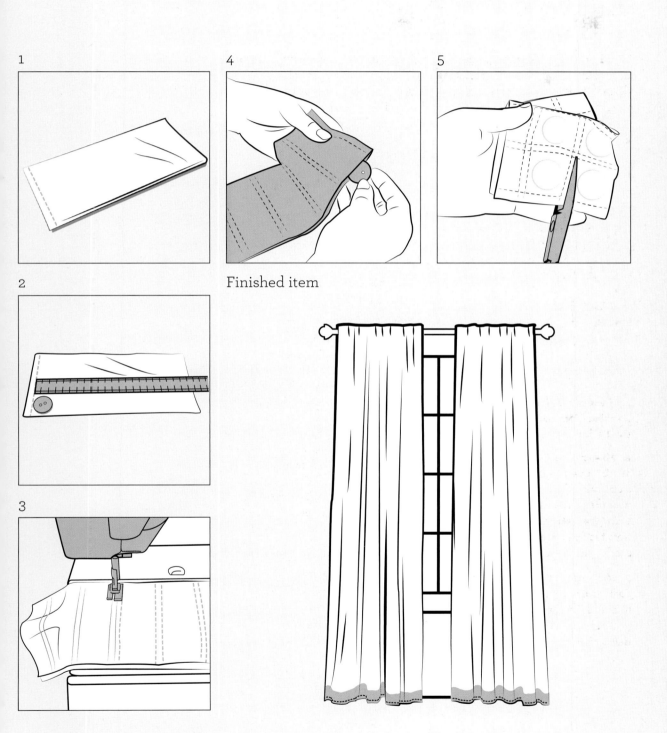

2

3

4

Finished item

5

# Tutorial
# Lined Curtains

It may sound daunting, but making lined curtains requires basic sewing skills. By adding a lining, your curtains will look instantly professional. The additional layer will block more light from entering the room, and the extra weight will allow your curtains to hang beautifully. In this example your curtains will have a visible hem at the base. If you prefer, you can hand stitch a blind hem at step 3 (see page 60).

## YOU WILL NEED
- Curtain fabric
- Lining fabric
- Tape measure
- Scissors
- Thread
- Sewing machine
- Pins
- Iron

**1.** Measure your windows and calculate the fabric quantities needed (see pages 44–45). Cut your drops, sew any fabric widths together with a ⅝in (1.5cm) seam allowance, and press open the seams. Repeat this process with the lining fabric. Make them both the same length, but make the lining fabric 4¾in (12cm) narrower.

**2.** Turn up the bottom edge of the lining fabric by 2.5in (7cm) and press. Turn another 2.5in (7cm), press again, and pin in place. This is what we will refer to as a double hem.

**3.** Machine stitch the hem close to the folded edge.

**4.** Turn up a 4in (10cm) double hem on the main curtain fabric and machine stitch in place, close to the folded edge. Press.

**5.** Lay your main fabric right-side up and then lay your lining on top, right-side down. Line up along one edge and position the stitched hems on both fabrics together. The lining should now be sitting 1¼in (3cm) up from the bottom of the main fabric.

**6.** Pin along the edge and machine stitch the fabric and lining together. Use a ⅝in (1.5cm) seam allowance.

**7.** Maneuver the lining on the opposite side to line up with the edge of the main fabric. Check that the stitch lines sit together and the lining is still 1¼in (3cm) up from the bottom of the main fabric. Pin and machine stitch with a ⅝in (1.5cm) seam allowance.

**8.** Turn the fabrics right sides out and lay flat with the lining facing up. Position so that there are equal amounts of main fabric visible on each side of the lining. Press flat.

**9.** For a neat finish, miter your bottom corners. Fold the corner underneath, press, and slip stitch in place (see page 60).

**10.** You should now be left with an open bottom and top. The hems of both the main and lining curtain will not be sewn. This enables the curtain to hang freely. Trim any excess lining at the top of your curtain. You are now ready to add a header (see pages 94–97).

## THE BAGGING TECHNIQUE
The technique for lining curtains is often referred to as "bagging." The bagging technique is also used for reversible curtains (see pages 78–79).

### TIP
For a more bespoke look, try using a lining fabric in a complementary color, or with a contrasting pattern, to your main fabric.

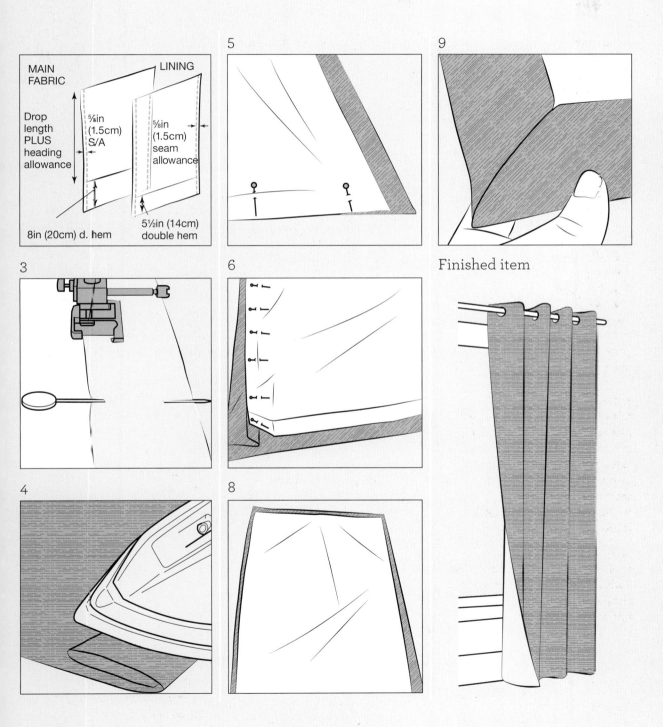

**MAIN FABRIC**

**LINING**

Drop length PLUS heading allowance

⅝in (1.5cm) S/A

⅝in (1.5cm) seam allowance

8in (20cm) d. hem

5½in (14cm) double hem

5

9

3

6

Finished item

4

8

# Tutorial
# Reversible Curtains

In addition to lined curtains, the bagging technique can be employed to make reversible curtains. At its simplest, the two main fabrics are hemmed, sewn together face-to-face to form a bag, then turned inside out. Whether you do actually turn your curtains with the seasons or not, the use of a complementary fabric on the reverse is great for adding interest to your window treatments. This method works well with tab tops (as in this example), eyelets, or clips.

## YOU WILL NEED
- Fabric for both sides of the curtain
- Measuring tape
- Scissors
- Thread
- Sewing machine
- Pins
- Curtain pole
- Iron

**1.** To begin, select your fabrics for the two sides of the curtain and cut to the same width and length, adding 1¼in (3cm) to the width and ⅝in (1.5cm) at the top. Add a further 8in (20cm) to the length for the hem. The finished length of your curtains will depend on how long you want the curtain and tabs to be. If you need to join fabric to make up the width, use a ⅝in (1.5cm) seam allowance. Turn up a 4in (10cm) double hem on each piece of fabric. Press and machine stitch close to the fold. Set both panels to one side.

**2.** For the tap tops, cut equal strips of front and back fabrics. I've cut them 7in (18cm) long and 4in (10cm) wide. I think the best way to work this out is pretty hands-on, and will depend on your personal taste. Cut a tab 4in (10cm) wide and wrap over your curtain pole. Add 1¼in (3cm) for your seam allowances and a further 2in (5cm) so that it's not too tight to the pole. For more information on tab tops, see pages 84–85.

**3.** Sew the strips right sides together along each side of the long edge. Use a ⅝in (1.5cm) seam allowance. Make sure you start and finish with a reverse stitch.

**4.** Turn through and press flat. With this reversible curtain, you'll need to step the tabs in by ⅝in (1.5cm) at both sides of the curtain.

**5.** Lay out one of your curtain panels face-up. Fold the tab in half with the favored side facing outward. Line up the raw edges of the tabs with the raw edge of the top of the curtain panel. Step the tab in by ⅝in (1.5cm) on both sides. Pin together.

**6.** With all the tabs evenly spaced along the top of your curtain, machine stitch together with a ⅜in (1cm) seam allowance. The purpose is to secure the tabs before stitching the opposite panel. You may choose to hand tack. Whichever method you choose, the aim is to hold the tabs in position before you sew everything together.

**7.** Place your second curtain panel facedown on top of the first panel and the tabs. Line up the raw edges at the top and the sides. Pin together and machine stitch with a ⅝in (1.5cm) seam allowance.

**8.** Snip the corners at an angle to reduce bulk and create a crisper finish. Similarly, you can snip the seam allowance at the bottom corners so that there are no raw edges visible. Turn out and press the edges flat. Run the curtain pole through the tabs and hang.

### TIP
Remember, fabric will fade in the sunlight. Because of the nature of the drape, it also fade in stripes, so choose the two fabrics for your reversible curtains with this in mind.

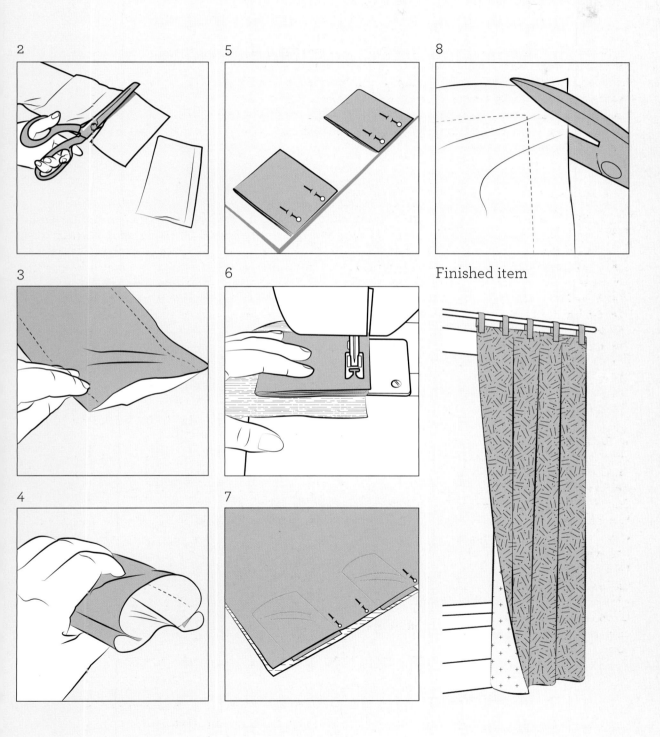

2

5

8

3

6

Finished item

4

7

# Tutorial
# Working with Sheer Fabrics

Sheer curtains are great for privacy or blocking an unsightly view without plunging a room into darkness. The light that passes through them is softened; combine this with the movement created by a drafty window and there you are in your very own romantic film set. Silks, chiffon, voile, and organza are classed as sheers, and as a group can be pretty tricky to work with. Here are a few techniques for the taming of the sheer!

## CUTTING AND HANDLING

To get an accurate straight line for cutting sheers, try pulling a thread.

**1.** Mark where you need to make a cut and snip the fabric.

**2.** Tease out a thread and pull while holding the fabric.

**3.** Break the thread and flatten out the fabric. There will now be a thread missing, which will be easy to follow with scissors.

Another method of marking and cutting is to weigh down the fabric. Place a cutting mat on the table with the sheer fabric on top and clamp in place, then use a metal ruler and a sharp rotary cutter or craft knife to cut the fabric.

If you find the fabric is fraying uncontrollably, apply some liquid seam sealant to the edges.

## STITCHING

Any stitching you apply to sheer fabric will be visible from both sides of the curtain. Take your time when feeding through the machine. Test on a scrap piece of fabric first, and use a smaller needle, a shorter stitch length, and some fine thread. It might also be advisable to adjust the tension—refer to your sewing machine manual. You can also replace the sewing machine's needle or change the throat plate for a single hole plate. This will cause minimal pulling of the fabric as the needle passes through it.

Before you start sewing, place a piece of tissue paper under and on top of the fabric. This can be ripped off once stitching is complete. Hold the fabric flat and taut at the front and back of the machine as you sew (see image 3).

Pins can easily mark or pull threads in sheer fabrics, so it's best to work with fine silk pins.

## JOINING USING FRENCH SEAMS

French seams are particularly good for sheer fabrics, as they enclose raw edges that fray easily.

**1.** Place the fabric with the wrong sides facing. Machine stitch ¼in (6mm) from the raw edge and press the seam open (I find this helps with step 2).

**2.** Turn the fabric so that the right sides are facing. Machine stitch ⅜in (1cm) from the seamed edge to enclose the raw edges (see image 4).

## FINISHING

Sheers can be finished in many different ways. The most important thing to remember is that any stitching will be seen from both sides of the fabric. Commonly, you see sheers finished with tab tops or a ruched casing. There are also transparent heading tapes on the market if you're after a more traditional pleat.

Think about the length of the curtain. Sheers can look great with the bottom of the curtain puddled—gathered on the floor in a pile. If you want the curtains to hang short of the floor, it might be worth adding sausage-style drapery weights into the bottom hem. See pages 74–75 for information about adding weights.

## Cutting and handling

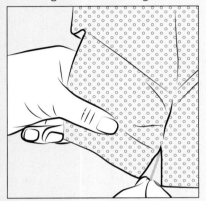

## Joining using French seams

## Cutting and handling

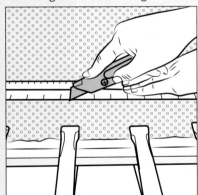

## Finished item

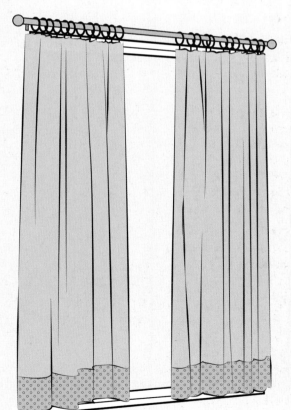

## Stitching

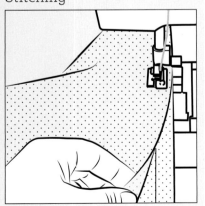

# Tutorial
# Weighted Sheer Curtains

Here's a simple sheer curtain with a casing top. The curtain can be kept flat or gathered on the pole, so work out the fullness of the curtain you require (see page 46). If you need to join widths, use a French seam, as described on page 62.

**2**

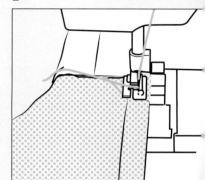

## YOU WILL NEED
- Sheer fabric
- Sewing machine
- Fine needles and thread
- Rotary cutter
- Metal ruler
- Silk pins (or the finest you can find)
- Sausage lead weights
- Needle for hand stitching
- Safety pin

**3.** Measure up from the bottom of the curtain to the desired drop. Turn back the 4in (10cm) casing allowance and turn in a further ⅜in (1cm). Stitch together.

**4.** Thread the sausage lead weight through the bottom hem.

**5.** Using a matching thread, hand stitch the weights to the curtain fabric to hold them in place. Hand stitch the ends closed.

**6.** Feed the curtain pole through the casing and hang. Et voilà!

**1.** Measure up from the bottom of the curtain to the desired drop. In this case, it's the top of the pole. As I'm using drapery weights, I'll be stopping about ¾in (2cm) from the floor. Add 1½in (4cm) for a double bottom hem, plus 4⅜in (11cm) to the top for the casing. Cut the fabric.

**2.** Stitch the curtain panel to the desired width using a narrow double side hem.

**4**

## Finished item

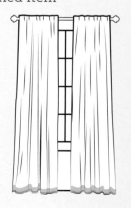

**Opposite:** Gap Interiors/Douglas Gibb

# Tutorial
# Tab Top Curtains

Tab tops add a decorative element to simple ungathered curtains. The use of contrasting fabric for the tabs, or the addition of decorative buttons, brings a bit of added interest to your window treatment. Although it might seem strange, tab tops work best in situations where the curtains are likely to remain closed! When closed, the tabs are neat and evenly spaced. When open, they bunch up next to each other, preventing the curtain from opening fully. With this in mind, think about installing a longer pole.

## YOU WILL NEED
- Curtain fabric
- Fabric for tabs
- Fabric for facing
- Scissors
- Sewing machine
- Matching thread
- Needle
- Pins
- Iron

## MEASUREMENTS
Typically, tabs are between 2–2½in (5–7cm) wide. Heavier-weight fabrics will require wider tabs, whereas more lightweight fabrics can be supported using much narrower tabs. The space between tabs is between one and three times the width of the tab, depending on how you want your curtains to hang. If you want to have a wider gap, the fabric needs to have a strong structure so that it doesn't bag.

When considering the length of a tab, it really is about the bigger picture. How big is the window? How long are the curtains? Make the tab length and width in proportion to the curtain.

**1.** Make up the over-length unlined curtain panels (see pages 72–73 for instructions). Turn in the sides and bottom hem and machine stitch.

**2.** To make the tabs, measure and cut some fabric to the required length and twice the required width, adding a 1¼in (3cm) seam allowance to both measurements. In this example the finished tabs are 6in (15cm) long and 2in (5cm) wide when finished, so I'm cutting 7¼in (18cm) x 5¼in (13cm) (remember, you'll need to multiply the width by two to take the folding in step 3 into account).

**3.** Fold the tabs in half lengthwise, right sides together. Machine stitch down the length with a ⅝in (1.5cm) seam allowance and then press the seam open.

**4.** Turn the tabs right side out.

**5.** Press each tab with the seam running down the center line.

**6.** Lay the curtain panel flat, right-side up, and measure from the bottom of the hem to the required drop length. Mark with pins. Measure another ⅝in (1.5cm) beyond the pins and trim to length.

**7.** Fold the tabs in half so the seam is on the inside. Position a tab at the edge of the curtain, with its raw ends lining up with the raw top of the curtain. The fold of the tab will be facing down the curtain. Pin in place. Secure another tab at the opposite end, evenly space the remaining tabs between them, and stitch in place ⅜in (1cm) from the raw edge.

**8.** To create a heading for the curtain, cut a piece of fabric the width of the curtain plus 1¼in (3cm) for seam allowances, and 7in (18cm) deep. Press back the edges and stitch ⅝in (1.5cm) hems on the two short sides and along one long side.

**9.** Match the raw edge of the panel with the raw edges of the curtain and tabs. Pin everything together with the right sides facing. Machine stitch with a ⅝in (1.5cm) seam allowance along the raw ends. Press open the seam.

**10.** Fold the top over so the wrong sides are together and the tabs are sticking out. Pin and slip stitch down the sides and along the open length.

2

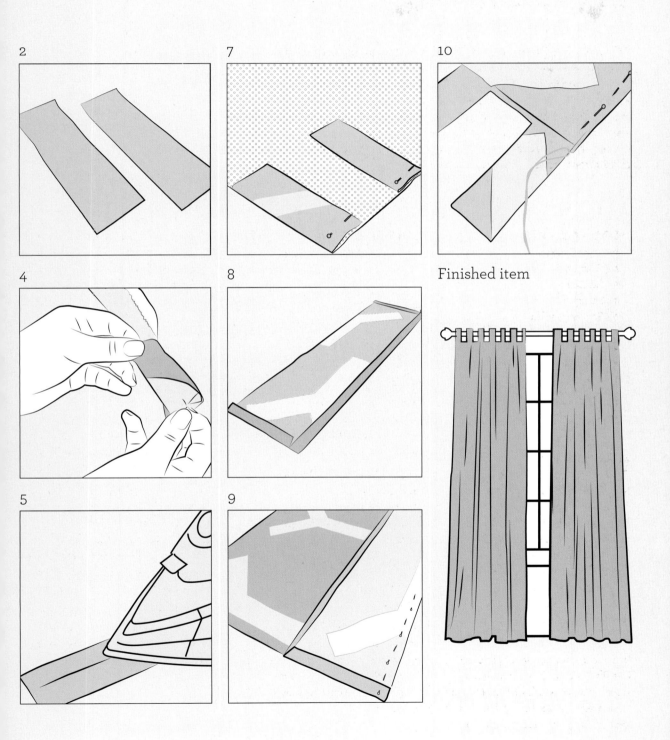

7

10

4

8

Finished item

5

9

# Tutorial
# Decorative Tab Top Curtains

Of course, curtain tabs needn't always be concealed—why not add a more decorative detail to the finished curtain instead? In the following tutorial I'm shaping the ends of the tabs, securing them to the face of the curtain panel, and finishing with decorative buttons.

## YOU WILL NEED

- Curtain fabric
- Fabric for tabs
- Fabric for facing
- Scissors
- Sewing machine
- Matching thread
- Buttons
- Needle
- Pins
- Iron

**1.** Follow step 1 on page 84. Make the tabs as in steps 2 and 3, but make them 2in (5cm) longer. Machine stitch along one of the short edges before turning right side out. This end will be seen, so be sure to turn out and press neatly. You can opt to make a pointed rather than a square end.

**2.** Continue to follow steps 4–6. At step 7, leave the tabs in a strip rather than folding. Line up the raw edges, pin in place, and continue to make the curtain to step 12.

**3.** Bring the long end of the tabs down over the front of the curtain. Carefully pin along the top curtain line.

**4.** Fold back the loose end of the tab and slip stitch the inside of the tab to the top of the curtain panel. This will prevent any pulling around the button in the following step.

**5.** Hand stitch a button, or something similar, in the center of the tabs to hold all of the layers together. Hang the curtains in place.

**TIP**
When choosing buttons for your tab tops, be creative. Think about using buttons in contrasting colors, or sewing them on with brightly colored thread. Thrift shops are also a great place to find more unusual and vintage buttons.

2

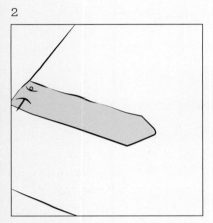

5

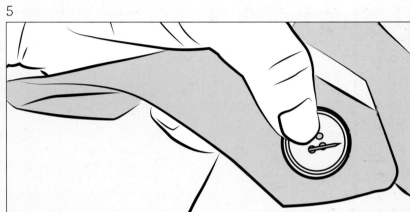

Finished item

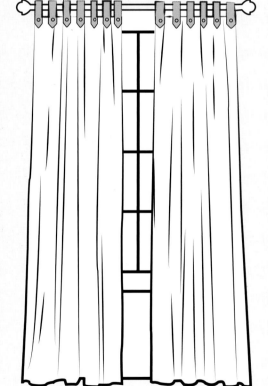

3

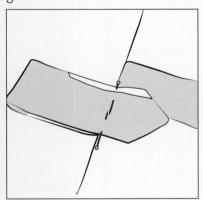

4

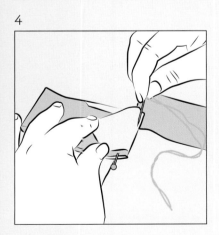

# Tutorial
# Tie Top Curtains

Once you've mastered the basic principles of making tab top curtains, there's nothing stopping you from experimenting—simply sewing pairs of longer tabs together will give you tie tops! In this example I'm making the ends of the ties into a point to add a bit of interest, and topstitching the ties to a simply hemmed panel. You could also opt for contrasting thread as a special feature. The drop length for tie top curtains won't be as precise as with other curtains, as you can adjust the length with the ties.

## YOU WILL NEED

- Curtain fabric
- Fabric for your ties
- Tailor's chalk or fabric pen
- Sewing machine
- Ruler
- Thread
- Scissors
- Iron

**1.** Begin by cutting out a basic unlined curtain panel. Cut the fabric with 2⅛in (6cm) extra for side hems, 2⅛in (6cm) for the top hem, and 6in (15cm) for a double bottom hem. Turn in the sides by ⅝in (1.5 cm) and press, then turn in again and topstitch. Turn up the bottom by 3in (7.5cm), press, and turn up a further 3in (7.5cm) and topstitch. Turn down the top by ⅝in (1.5cm), press, then turn down a further 1¾in (4.5cm) and topstitch.

**2.** For each tie, cut strips of the same fabric 4in (10cm) wide by 27½in (70cm) long. The number of ties you will need is the same in principal as for tab top curtains (see Measurements on page 84).

**3.** On the wrong side of the tab fabric, mark a faint center line down the length of each strip with a fabric pen or tailor's chalk.

**4.** Press in the corners at the ends of each tie to form points. The top edge of the fabric strip will now sit along the center line.

**5.** Trim back the folded ends made in step 4 to ¼in (6mm), then fold in ¼in (6mm) along the long edges and press flat.

**6.** Fold the ties in half lengthwise, so that the wrong sides are together. Press and pin together.

**7.** Topstitch all of the ties close to the edge.

**8.** Fold the ties in half and position and pin in place on the wrong side of the curtain panel.

**9.** Neatly machine stitch the ties to the curtain top in a square. Machine across the square to make a cross. Continue stitching the ties along the curtain and hang in place.

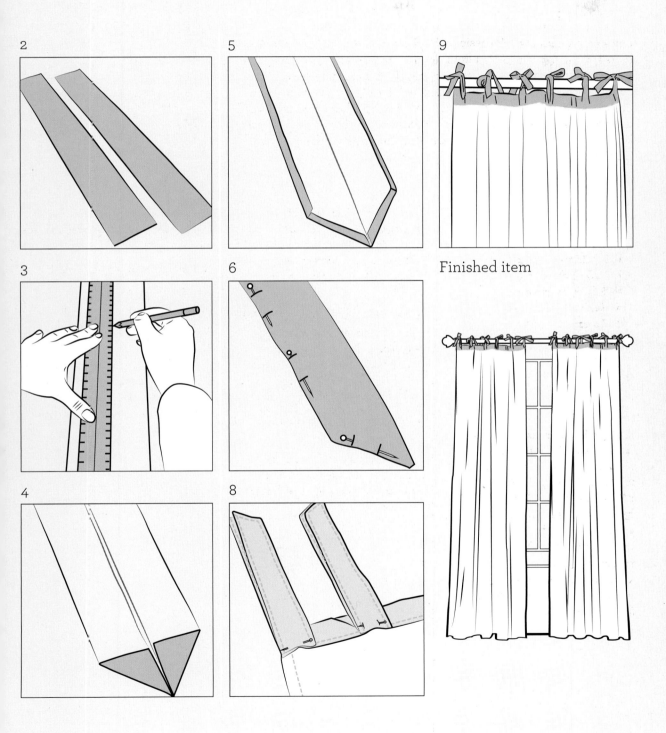

2

5

9

3

6

Finished item

4

8

# Tutorial
# Eyelet Curtains

Eyelet curtains are essentially curtain panels with holes that are reinforced with metal or plastic so that a curtain pole can fit through. Visually, I find myself drawn to the eyelet, so make sure to choose a finish that fits with your overall room scheme. Luckily, there are many eyelet tapes on the market with differing eyelet finishes and sizes, so you should be able to find something you like.

## YOU WILL NEED
- Eyelet tape
- Eyelets
- Curtain fabric
- Lining fabric
- Craft knife
- Pins
- Sewing machine
- Thread
- Scissors
- Clamps
- Ruler
- Cutting mat

**1.** Work out the finished drop length for your curtain panel. With eyelet curtains, this is the top of the pole. Add on the amount of fabric you want above the pole, multiply by two, and add the eyelet tape width plus extra for turning. Make up a lined curtain panel (see pages 76–77), leaving the top edge raw.

**2.** Place the curtain panel with the right side facing up. Mark the finished curtain drop length with pins at the top of the curtain.

**3.** Lay your eyelet tape along the top of the curtain. I want to have 1½in (4cm) of fabric sitting above the pole, so I'm positioning the tape 3in (8cm) up from the drop line. Position the tape so that there is an equal distance between the sides and the first and last hole. Leaving the pull cords free, cut the tape so there is about ⅜in (1cm) of tape over each edge for turning.

**4.** Pin the eyelet tape in place. Remove the pins from step 2.

**5.** Fold under the edges of the tape and pin. Leave a small gap between the folded edge and the curtain edge so that the tape is not visible from the front. Make sure the pull cords that run through the tape are left loose and not folded under.

**6.** Machine stitch along the top edge (the edge facing the curtain) of the tape. Stitch the sides, leaving the cords free. To prevent twisting, machine stitch along the bottom edge in the same direction as the top edge.

**7.** Remove the drop point pins. Turn the curtain over so that the right side is facing down. Fold the top of the curtain over so that the eyelet tape is once again visible. Measure so that the top of the eyehole is 1½in (4cm) from the fold. The top of the eyehole will now be at your original drop point mark from step 2.

1

Extra for turning

Eyelet tape

1½in (4cm)
Fold
1½in (4cm)

Fabric above pole

Top of pole

2

3

5

6

7

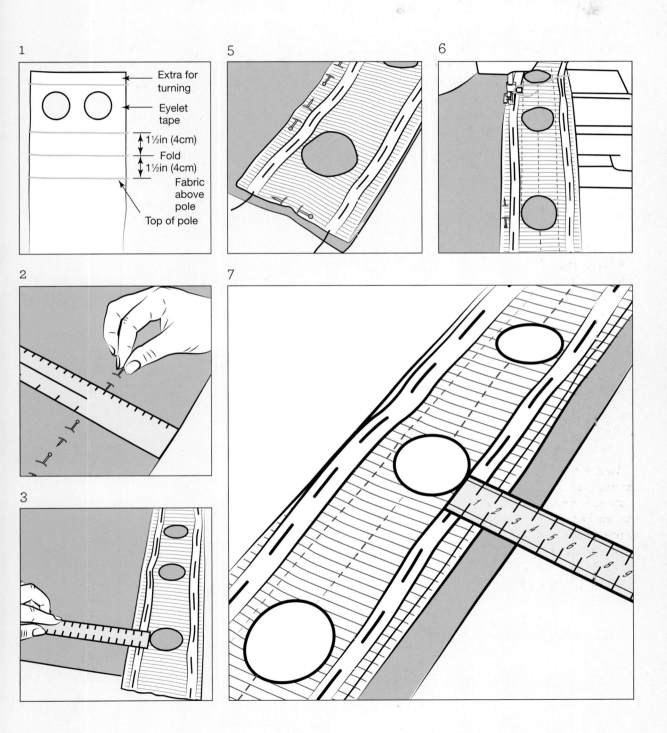

# Tutorial
# Eyelet Curtains continued

**8.** Turn under any raw ends of fabric and pin in place. You can now choose whether to hand stitch the eyelet tape to the lining fabric or machine stitch. Stitch again down the sides of the eyelet tape to enclose the fold.

**9.** Make sure the curtain is flat, and pin the tape to the curtain fabric around each eyelet hole.

**10.** Place a cutting mat under the curtain and clamp both to the table. Cut the eyelets using a craft knife. Whether you use a knife or scissors will depend on your cutting skills and the fabric. It's best to practice on a scrap piece of fabric first. Repeat for all the holes.

**11.** Slide the front half of the eyelet under the curtain and position the eyelet over the hole. Snap the back of the eyelet in place.

**12.** Pull the tape cords to shape the curtain. Tie a knot at both ends to hold the curves in place. Run the pole through the eyelet holes and hang.

8

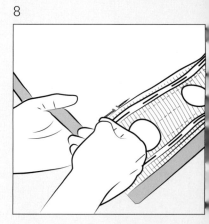

9

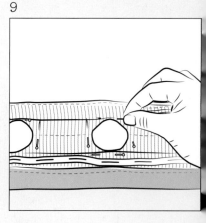

10

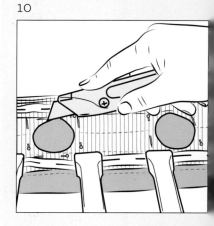

**11**

**12**

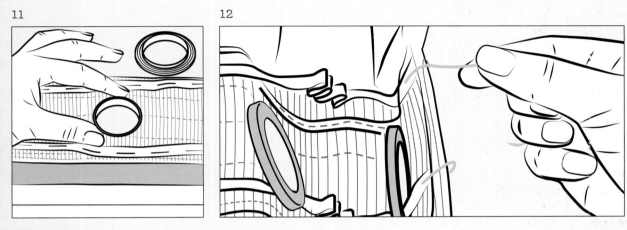

Finished item

# Tutorial
# Using Heading Tape

Heading tape comes in a variety of styles and helps to create pleat formations, in most cases removing the need for lengthy hand stitching. The tapes serve a triple function—stiffening the curtain heading, allowing easy gathering with cords, and providing pockets for curtain hooks to enable easy hanging. Choosing a heading tape style is as important as choosing your fabric, so do some research and think about the final look you want to achieve before buying.

## YOU WILL NEED

- Pencil pleat heading tape
- Curtain panel
- Sewing machine
- Thread
- Scissors
- Pins
- Ruler

## HEADING STYLES

- **Pencil pleats:** The most common pleat. Each pleat is shaped like an even row of pencils.
- **Pinch pleats:** Creates a more formal finish. Pleats are made in groups of three and spaced evenly between flat areas of fabric.
- **Box pleats:** Creates a more tailored, boxy finish (see pages 124–125 for making box pleats by hand).
- **Smock tape:** Best used with plain fabrics to show off the intricate smock detail.

The drop point for a header-taped curtain is the eyelet on the curtain ring. In this example, the fabric above the drop point covers the eyelet, leaving the curtain ring exposed.

## CREATING A PENCIL PLEAT HEADING

**1.** Work out the finished drop length for your curtain panel. With heading tape, this is from the curtain ring eyelet to the finished bottom of your curtain. Above the drop point add enough fabric for the header, multiply by two, and add the width of your tape plus ⅝in (1.5cm). Fold back your header and pin through the drop point so you can see the pin on the back of the curtain.

**2.** To establish the header tape position, put a curtain hook in the header tape, and position the tape so that the top of the hook aligns with the drop point. If there is a choice of hook pockets, choose the one that positions the top of the tape closest to the header fold—this helps to keep the header firm.

**3.** Cut the tape to the width of each curtain, plus an extra 2in (5cm) on each side.

**4.** Lay the tape in the selected position with the hook pockets facing up. Pull about 2in (5cm) of cord out of the tape on both sides of the curtain. Securely knot each cord on the leading edge.

**5.** Trim the excess tape to about 1in (2.5cm) on the leading edge (the edge of the curtain nearest the center of the window) and turn under, cords included. Pin the tape in place. Repeat for the outer edge of the curtain, but leave the cords free. Make sure there is a hook pocket close to each end of the curtain.

### TIP
You can also add heading tape in the same way as eyelet tape. Use whichever method works best for you.

Some tapes are more suitable for different fabrics. Always check with your supplier.

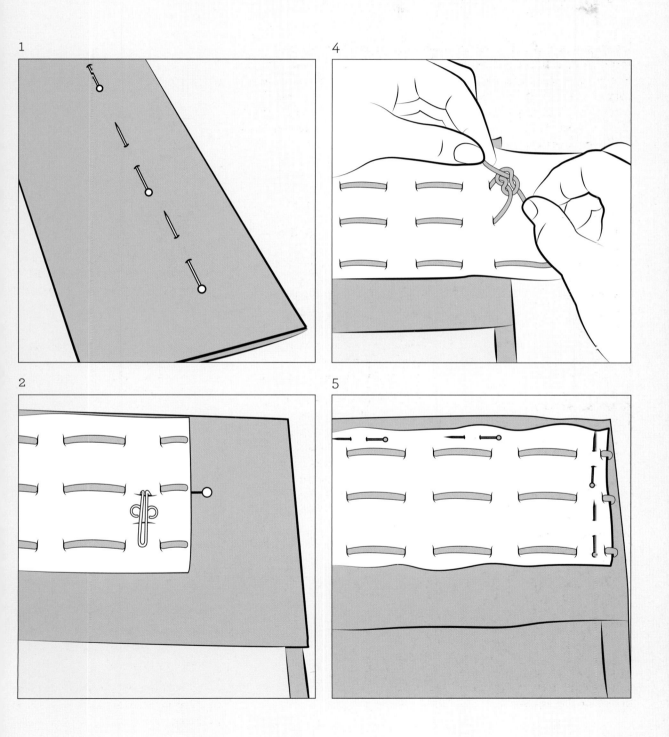

# Tutorial
# Using Heading Tape continued

**6.** Straight-stitch the tape to the curtain, close to the edges. Start at the bottom left-hand corner, stitch up the side, along the top, and down the opposite side. Turn under the raw edges of the curtain and lining fabric and stitch the bottom of the tape from the original start point. Note that you need to stitch in the same direction along the top and the bottom to prevent any twisting. Don't stitch over the cords on the outer edge of the curtain.

**7.** Securely hold onto the free ends of the cords with one hand. With your other hand, gently push the heading tape along the cords, away from the loose ends, so that the fabric is pleated to the maximum extent and the pleats are set.

**8.** Ease the end of the heading out again until the curtain is the correct width. Tie a slipknot in the loose cords. Do not cut the cords—the heading tape will need to be pulled back out if the curtains ever need to be stored or cleaned. Work the pleats along the flattened tape again until even.

**9.** Insert a curtain hook in the first and last pocket on the tape. Space the remaining hooks evenly apart—about 4in (10cm) is a good distance.

**10.** Tidy up the loose cords on the outer curtain edge. Bring the cords through the knot, but stop short of bringing them completely through. You will now have a loop shape.

**11.** Twist the loop together until the cords start to buckle. Double back the end of the cord and they will form into a twisted roll. Feed the roll into the heading tape so that it is neatly stored away.

**12.** Bring the curtain to the pole and feed the hooks through the eye of the curtain rings.

**13.** To train the folds in the curtains, dress the pleats down their length and pull the curtains back together. Do this by tying a scrap piece of fabric around the whole curtain in a couple of places—but don't tie so tight that you leave indentation marks in the fabric! Leave like this for two or three days and then remove the scrap fabric.

---

**TIP**

If using velvet, don't fold and tie the curtains at step 13. If you do, the ties will permanently mark the fabric as it flattens the nap.

**7**

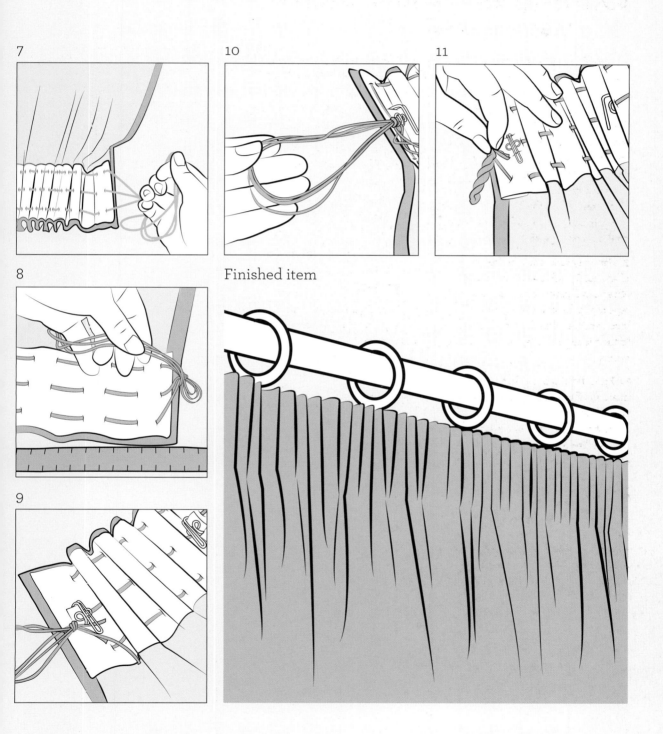

**10**

**11**

**8**

Finished item

**9**

# Case Study
# Will Taylor, Bright Bazaar

Will Taylor is a blogger and interiors journalist with two addictions—one for color and another for colorful bow ties! He launched his award-winning blog, *Bright Bazaar*, in 2009, and by 2014 his first book, *Bright Bazaar: Embracing Color for Make-You-Smile Style*, hit the shelves.

If you follow *Bright Bazaar*, you may have noticed that Will's apartment was bright and airy, with beautifully tall windows. When he moved in, the windows were covered in "horrific" office blinds: "Needless to say, I whipped those monstrous things out quickly!" says Will. The hunt for ready-made curtains big enough to fit the windows proved tricky. Forever positive, Will saw this as an opportunity to choose fabric that would fit his aesthetic. "So of course, I went for the cheeriest yellow fabric I could find! I fell hard and fast for Vanessa Arbuthnott's French Ticking design." Will is clearly a fan of stripes, and offers some useful advice when it comes to incorporating them into the home: "Introduce stripes in varying sizes and shades, but stick to the same color family for a coordinated look."

Sewing machine at the ready, fabric and lining pressed, Will set about making the curtains. Each curtain was made up using one and a half widths of fabric and lining. Having joined the fabric widths, Will turned and pressed the hems. He then pinned the lining behind the folded hems and ran each side through the machine. To hang, Will clipped Ikea curtain hooks to the reverse of the top hem. The clips give

*"Introduce stripes in varying sizes and shades, but stick to the same color family for a coordinated look."*

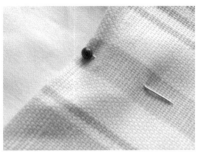

a similar visual effect to heading tape, but are much simpler to apply. Describing the final result, Will says, "I'm so pleased with how they turned out—the linen gives them a tactile feel and the yellow brings so much vibrancy and energy to the room."

**BRIGHT BAZAAR**
www.brightbazaarblog.com

**LIVES**
London, UK

**WINDOW TREATMENT STYLE**
Full-length lined curtains

**FABRIC USED**
"French Ticking—Buttercup and Clay" by Vanessa Arbuthnott (60% linen, 40% organic cotton)

**SIMILAR TUTORIALS**
Lined Curtains, pages 76–77

# Curtains and Drapes
## Gallery

**Left:** Gap Interiors/Bruce Hemming. **Top:** Dovilé Cavina/
Lovely Home Idea. **Bottom:** Calle Macarone/Callemac.
**Opposite:** Ashley McLeod/Domestic Imperfection.

# CHAPTER 6

## Blinds

# Overview

Making your own blinds is much the same as curtain making, just with the addition of cords and ties needed for operation. This seemingly convoluted mechanism can easily scare off the most experienced sewer, but the system itself is very basic. The Roll-up Blinds tutorial (see pages 106–107) shows you how to make the blind and the system—it's really very simple! If you still find the cords daunting, make the roll-up blinds using fabric ties, or even belts, to hold the blinds open. Even if you choose to use a store-bought kit, making your own blinds is cost-effective and incredibly rewarding. Measure accurately and take your time. Have fun with fabrics and add trimmings for a more bespoke feel.

**Opposite:** Gap Interiors/Tria Giovan

# Tutorial
# Measuring for Blinds

Measuring for blinds is relatively straightforward; however, you need to think about how you want the blind to look and what it needs to do. Before measuring, you'll need to decide whether you are hanging the blind inside or outside the window recess.

## INSIDE

Blinds set within the window recess can look neat and unobtrusive. It is generally best to avoid styles such as Roman blinds, which will block out light even when fully open; roller or venetian blinds often work well as they are compact when drawn up. You will need to consider whether the blind will interfere with the window catches and locks, or even stop the window from opening. Measuring the height of the recess is straightforward, but always take top, bottom, and middle measurements of the width in order to find the narrowest point. Make sure you allow enough room for the blind operating mechanism.

## OUTSIDE

Blinds fitted to the face of the wall above the recess can reveal the window fully and let in more light. They also tend to make the window appear larger. It is really a matter of personal taste as to how much you overlap the window, but 4in (10cm) on either side is standard—just watch out for light switches. If you're a fan of ornaments sitting on the windowsill, outside mounting is for you. Another general consideration is whether to have the mechanism on the left or right of the blind.

## HEALTH AND SAFETY

Make sure chains and other blind mechanisms are out of the reach of children.

### Measuring inside a recess

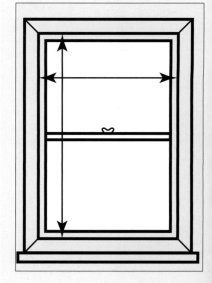

### Measuring outside a recess

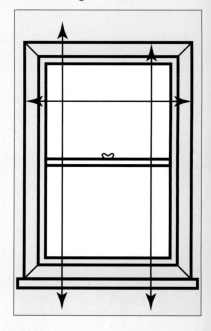

**Opposite:** Gap Interiors/Douglas Gibb

# Tutorial
# Roll-up Blinds

Roll-up blinds, also referred to as Swedish blinds, roll up using a system of cords. Although they're similar in principle to Roman blinds, the finished look is a little more casual. Both the face and reverse of the blind will be visible, so it's the perfect excuse to play with fabric color combinations. The cords are also on show, so think about all the elements and how they will work together. In this example, I've used the bagging technique to make the blind (see page 76).

## YOU WILL NEED
- A wood batten (to attach blind to wall)
- Screws
- Wall plugs
- 3 screw eyes
- Staples and staple gun
- Eyelet maker and eyelets
- Fabric for front of blind
- Fabric for back of blind
- Lining fabric to cover batten
- Cord
- Dowel
- Sewing machine
- Zipper foot
- Thread
- Pins
- Bradawl
- Pull cord weight
- Cleat
- Spirit level

**1.** Select a wood batten to hold your blind to the wall. Cut the batten ¼in (6mm) less than the finished width of the blind. Measure two sides of the batten—the side facing the ceiling and the side facing the wall. The batten I am using is 2in (5cm) by 1in (2.5cm). Make a note of this measurement.

**2.** The batten will be attached to the wall by two or more screws. Position the batten above the window and draw a line along the top. Use a spirit level to keep the batten straight. Drill two screw holes into either end of the batten. If your batten is quite long, add another screw hole. Bring the batten back to the window and line up with your drawn line. Use a pencil or screw to mark the wall through the screw holes. Drill and insert the wall plugs.

**3.** Cover the batten in lining fabric or a fabric of your choice, and secure in place using a staple gun. Locate the screw holes and make a hole through the fabric using a sharp instrument, such as a bradawl.

**4.** The blind will eventually have two cords visible from the front. Note: you may need additional cords down the center of the blind for wider windows. Think about how they will sit. Fit two screw eyes into the underside of the wood batten in the same position as where you would like the cords to go. Fit a third screw eye close to the right-hand end for operation at the right, or to the left-hand end for operation at the left.

**5.** Cut the front and back pieces of fabric the width of your window plus ¾in (2cm) and the drop (top of finished batten), plus the measurement taken in step 1. Add to this a further 4in (10cm). This will be for the roll of fabric that sits permanently at the bottom of the blind. Place both pieces right sides together, lining up the edges, and then stitch the bottom and sides together with a ⅜in (1cm) seam allowance.

## EYELET-MAKING KITS
There are many eyelet-making kits on the market: some very cheap and good, some very cheap and not so good! Buy from a reputable supplier.

## Roll-up blinds guide

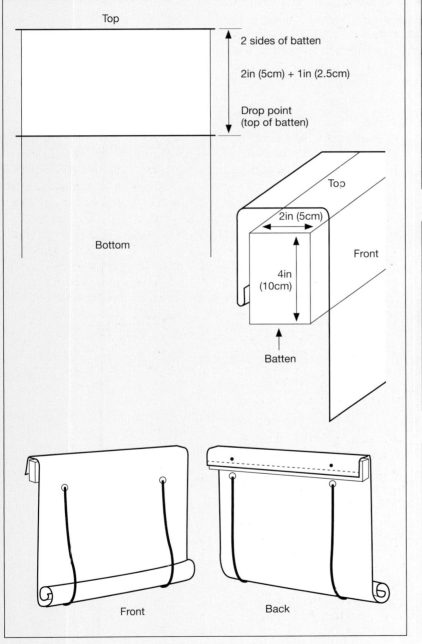

Top

2 sides of batten

2in (5cm) + 1in (2.5cm)

Drop point
(top of batten)

Bottom

Top

2in (5cm)

Front

4in
(10cm)

Batten

Front

Back

2

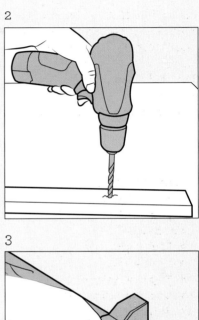

3

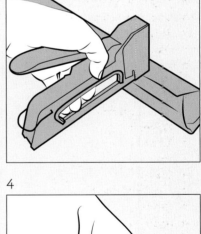

4

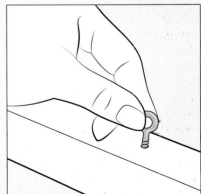

# Tutorial
# Roll-up Blinds continued

**6.** Cut the bottom corners across the diagonal to reduce bulk.

**7.** Turn the stitched panel with the right sides out.

**8.** Lay the blind panel right-side down. Measure up from the bottom of the blind to the finished drop length. Mark, fold, and press reverse sides together.

**9.** Measure and cut some dowel to the width of your blind minus ⅜in (1cm). A handy tip is to cover the cut line with masking tape before sawing—this will stop the dowel from splintering.

**10.** Put the dowel into the fabric bag and work it to the bottom.

**11.** Using a zipper foot on the sewing machine, stitch as close as possible to the dowel to hold it in place. If you don't have access to a zipper foot you can hand stitch close to the batten.

**12.** Position the top-facing corner of the batten into the top fabric fold from step 8. Wrap the surplus fabric over the top and down the back to the bottom edge. Make sure the batten is centered on the blind. The screw eyes should be facing down the length of the blind. Fold under the raw ends and staple the fabric to the batten.

**13.** Measure 2in (5cm) down the blind from the bottom of the batten. Place pins in line with the two screw eyes (but not under the third screw eye).

**14.** Make two eyelets at these points using an eyelet-making kit. Always practice on a scrap piece of fabric before committing to your blind. Lift up the front of the blind and screw the batten to the wall (it's much easier to get the levels of the cords right when the blind is hanging).

**15.** Thread the cords. Staple one end of the cord onto the batten behind the first screw eye. Pass the cord through the screw eye, down and under the bottom of the blind and back up the front. Pass the cord through the eyelet toward the back of the blind. Feed back through the screw eye and bring the cord over and through the third screw eye. Repeat this process for the second screw eye.

**16.** Attach a pull cord weight to the end of the cords and tie off to a cleat on the wall.

**17.** If you find the fabric bagging open as you raise the blind, add stab stitches at regular intervals up the blind. They will help to hold the two fabric panels together.

6

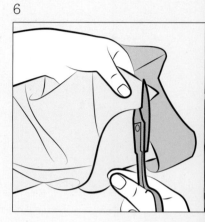

9

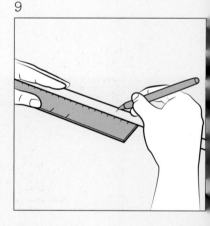

10

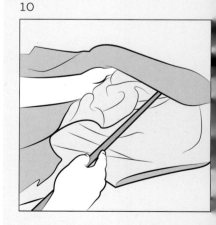

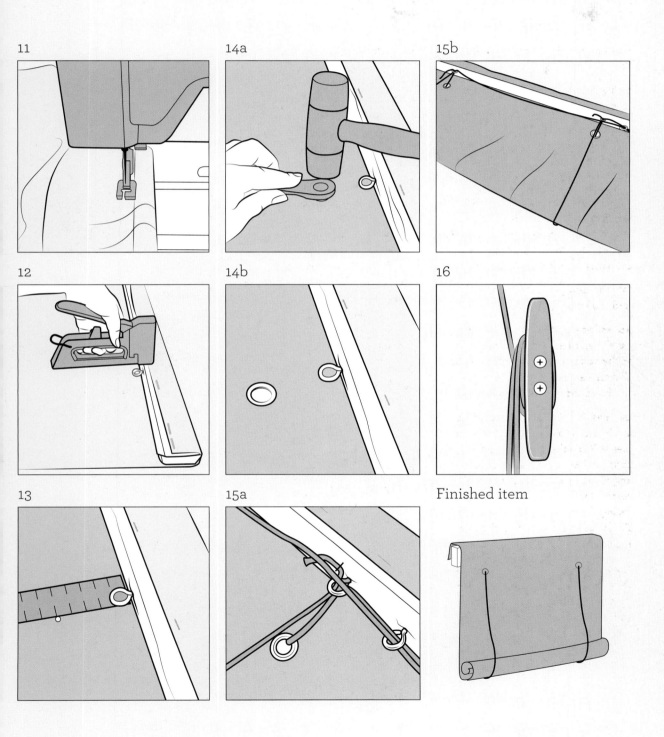

11

12

13

14a

14b

15a

15b

16

Finished item

# Tutorial
# Roman Blinds

I really like the simplicity of Roman blinds. The flat, folded pleats give the feel of a tailored curtain. The rise and fall system is the same in principle to a roll-up blind, but the finish is much more formal. Of course, the Roman blind needn't be stuffy—play with pattern, or add borders or alternating fabric for each pleat.

## BEFORE YOU GET STARTED

You will need to make a few decisions before making your blind. Think about the fabric. Folds of linen with no lining would be less crisp than, say, velvet. Heavier fabrics, and those with added interlining, will require a more robust system—buying a kit could be a better option than a homemade batten with screw eyes. Think also about the positioning of the blind. Do you want itto hang inside or outside the window recess? Remember, if positioned within the recess, the blind will still cover part of the window when raised.

## MEASURING AND CUTTING

As with curtain making, you'll need to measure the overall finished size of your blind. This will be from the top of the batten to the required length. To this measurement you'll need to add extra for the side and bottom hems and for the top of the blind. For the lining, you'll need to add extra for side and bottom hems and also extra for rod pockets.

## HERE ARE SOME CALCULATIONS TO DEMONSTRATE:

### Main fabric

Width is 35½in (90cm) + 3in (8cm) for turning = 38½in (98cm)

Length is 43in (110cm) + 8in (20cm) for hem and top = 51in (130cm)

### Lining fabric

Width: 35½in (90cm)

Length: 43in (110cm) + 6in (15cm) for hem and top + 1¼in (3cm) for each batten = 50¼in (128cm). Note that the hems are dependent on the size of the bottom rod, and the rod pockets are dependent on the size of the rods.

## CALCULATE THE PLEAT DIMENSIONS

43in (110cm) (finished drop—the top of batten to required length)

- 2in (5cm) (top of batten to bottom of cord guides) = 41in (105cm)

÷ 7 (the number of half-pleats—I have three battens so want seven half-pleats)

= 6in (15cm) for each half-pleat (refer to the diagram opposite for a guide)

## CASCADING FOLDS

Change the look of the blinds using different pleat sizes (see diagrams of cascade and standard Roman blinds opposite). Measure each pleat to be roughly 2in (5cm) more than the previous pleat to produce a cascade effect. The construction is the same, you just have to calculate the pleat spacing slightly differently. Measure how much of your window will be covered before making.

## Cascade blind

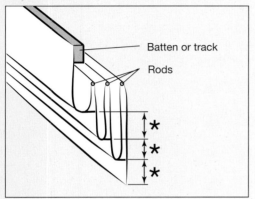

Batten or track

Rods

\* \* \*

## Standard Roman

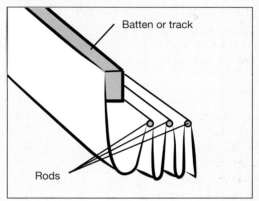

Batten or track

Rods

## Top of batten to bottom of cord guides

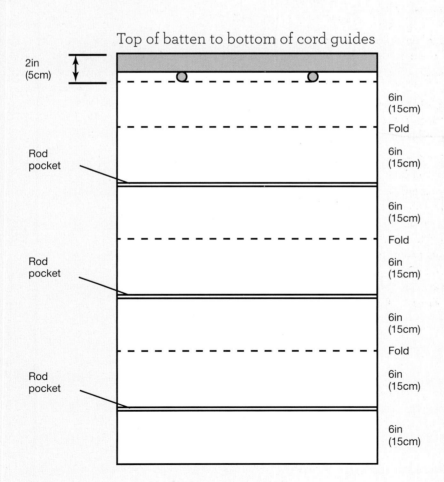

2in
(5cm)

Rod pocket

Rod pocket

Rod pocket

6in (15cm)

Fold

6in (15cm)

6in (15cm)

Fold

6in (15cm)

6in (15cm)

Fold

6in (15cm)

6in (15cm)

# Tutorial
# Roman Blinds continued

## YOU WILL NEED

- Fabric for the blind
- Lining fabric
- Scissors
- Tailor's chalk
- Pencil
- Ruler
- Set square
- Sewing machine
- Pins
- Needle
- Thread
- Iron
- Roman blind kit

## IF NOT USING A ROMAN BLIND KIT YOU WILL ALSO NEED

- Wood batten
- Screw eyes
- Cord
- Blind rings
- Sticky-backed Velcro
- Thin Roman blind rods
- Weighted bottom rod
- Wall plugs and screws for attaching to the wall

**1.** Position the main fabric right side facing down. Turn a double 1½in (4cm) side hem on both sides and press. Turn and press a double 2in (5cm) bottom hem. Measure from the bottom and mark the finished drop length at the top. Fold and iron, but don't stitch.

**2.** Secure the side hems using a serge stitch (see page 60). Put to one side. If you prefer, you can tuck some fusible webb under the fold and iron to secure in place.

**3.** All the trickier work goes into the lining fabric. With the right side facing down, turn a double 3¼in (2cm) side hem on both sides and press. To make a pocket for the bottom batten, turn up 2in (5cm), then turn under ⅜in (1cm). Press and machine stitch close to the last fold.

**4.** To make the dowel pockets, turn the lining over with the right side facing up and measure up a half-pleat from the bottom. In this case, mine is 6in (15cm). To make sure the line is perfectly horizontal, use a set square and ruler and draw a faint line across the lining. Be as accurate as possible.

**5.** Fold the half-pleat under along this line and press. Measure ⅝in (1.5cm) up from the fold and draw another line. Pin and machine stitch along this line. Note that most machines have a seam allowance guide, so you may not want to draw this line—it all depends on your confidence on the machine. Mark the next dowel pocket from the stitched line. This time the measurement is 12in (30cm). Fold, press, and stitch ⅝in (1.5cm) up from the fold again. Continue until all the dowel pockets are stitched.

**6.** Lay the main fabric facedown. Mark the positioning of the dowel pockets along the side hems with pins. In my case, the first dowel pocket is 6in (15cm) up from the bottom of the blind. My second pocket is marked 12in (30cm) up from the first, and so on.

**7.** Lay the lining fabric right-side up on top of the main fabric. The dowel pockets you made will be facing you. Position so that the lining is centered and lined up with the bottom of the main fabric. Line up the stitched lines of your dowel pockets with the marks or pins from step 6 on your main fabric. Pin the fabric panels together.

**8.** Open out the folded hem on the main fabric and slide the lining into the bottom of the fold. Fold the main fabric back over and pin. Machine stitch the layers together, close to the top of the fold.

2

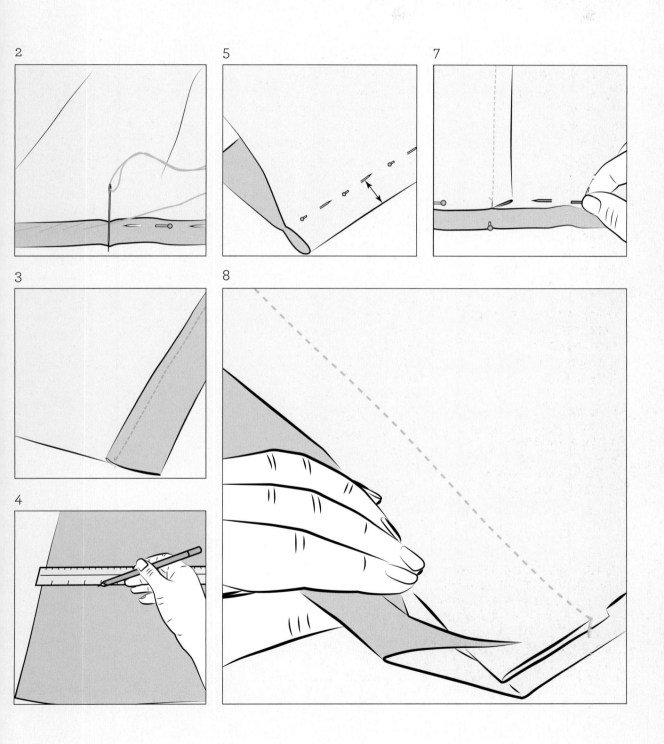

5

7

3

8

4

# Tutorial
# Roman Blinds continued

**9.** Using a matching thread, slip stitch (see page 60) the folded edge of the lining fabric to the main fabric by hand.

**10.** Keeping the fabric as flat as possible, pin along the stitched line of the dowel pockets, securing the lining and main fabric together.

**11.** Using a matching thread to your main fabric, evenly stab stitch (see page 60) the dowel pockets to the main fabric across the blind by hand.

**12.** Flatten out the blind and turn the top fold you made in step 1 over. Fold under the raw edge, press, and pin all the layers together. You may need to trim some of the lining fabric at this point. Position the soft side of the Velcro along the width of the blind just below the top. Pin and machine stitch the layers together. Stick the rough side of the Velcro to the track or batten. Attach the blind to the track using the Velcro.

**13.** Cut the rods for the pockets ⅜in (1cm) shorter than the width of the blind. Insert into the pockets and hand stitch the ends closed. Insert the weighted bottom rod into the bottom pocket of the lining fabric and hand stitch the ends closed.

**14.** Making sure the cord holders on the track are well spaced, mark the ring positions on each dowel pocket. Spacing will depend on the width of the blind, but in general 4–6in (10–15cm) is a good distance.

**15.** Attach the blind rings to the dowel pockets using a buttonhole stitch (see page 60).

**16.** Thread the cords down through the rings.

**17.** Lock the cords in position at the bottom with a slipknot, leaving enough free cord for the blind pull. Hang the blind in place.

**18.** Fix a cleat to the wall at a handy height and wrap the cords to secure.

9

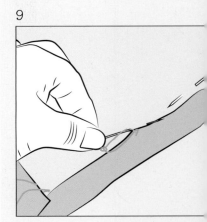

10

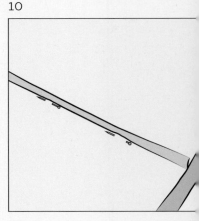

11

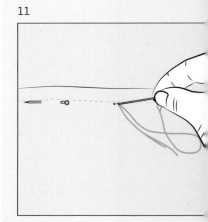

13

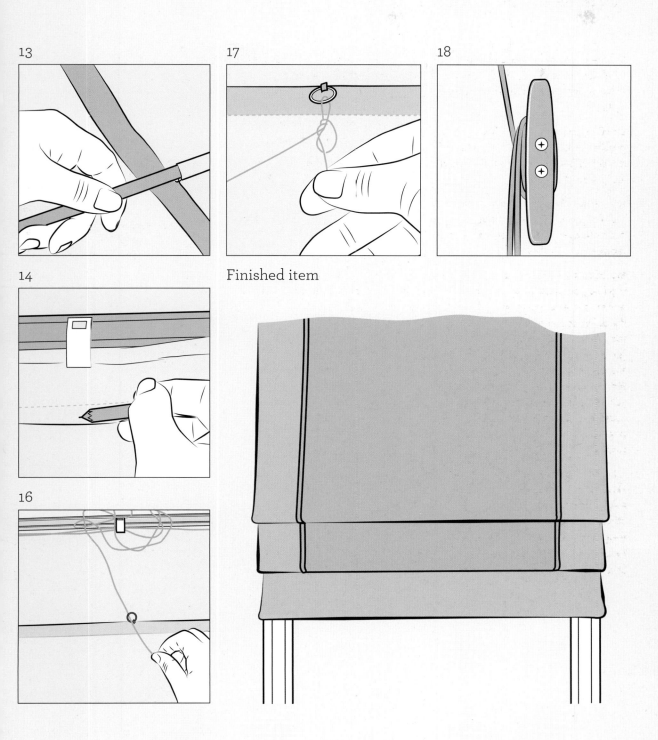

17

18

14

Finished item

16

# Tutorial
# Simple Rod Pockets

When it comes to unlined or bagged Roman blind panels, a simple shortcut can be used to make the rod pockets out of cotton twill tape. This is a great tip if you are unsure of your measuring and sewing skills.

## YOU WILL NEED

- Cotton twill tape
- Bagged or unlined panel
- Sewing machine
- Roman blind rods

**1.** Make up the blind panel. Turn in the hems for an unlined blind or use the bagging technique for lined blinds (see page 76).

**2.** Lay the blind right-side down. Measure and mark the positioning of the dowel pockets (see page 110 for more information on pleat dimensions).

**3.** For the rod pockets, cut strips of twill tape a touch shorter than the width of the finished blind. This will ensure no tape is visible when the blind is hung.

**4.** Iron each piece of tape in half lengthwise.

**5.** Keeping the blind right-side down, position the twill tape pockets along the marks made in step 2. The raw edges of the twill tape should be placed along the lines, with the fold facing the bottom of the blind.

**6.** Machine stitch the tape onto the blind, keeping close to the raw edges.

**7.** Cut the rods slightly shorter than the width of the blind and feed them into the twill pockets.

**8.** Hand stitch the ends of the rod pockets closed. Follow steps 14–18 on page 114 to finish the blind.

### TIP

Make sure your dowel pockets are evenly spaced, so that the pleats are uniform when you pull up your shade. If you place your dowels too close together, the shade will bunch when opened, and if they are too far apart, the fabric will sag.

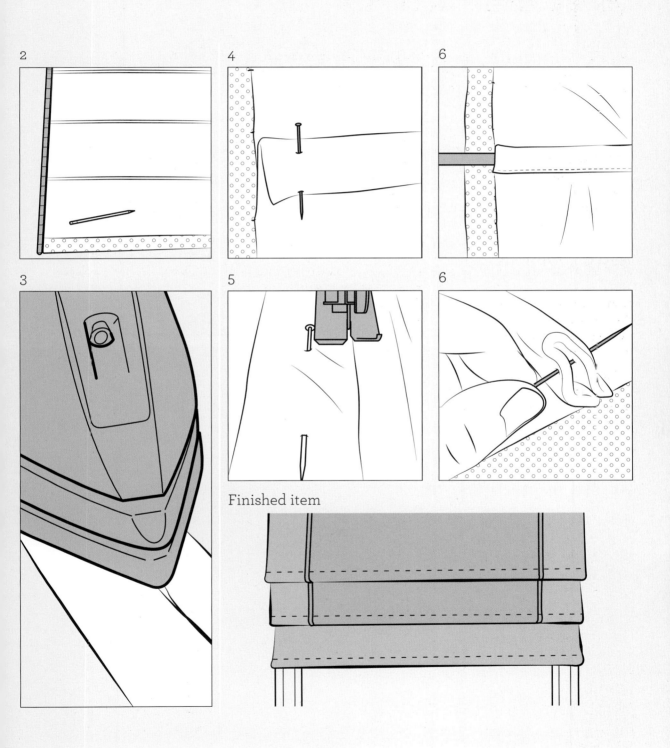

2

3

4

5

6

6

Finished item

# Case Study
# Lisa Barrett, Tango & James

Lisa Barrett is a prolific designer and chair rescuer, upholstering mainly retro chairs with her own vibrant fabrics. After studying fashion, textiles, and interior design, Lisa spent a few years perfecting her style, designing and making handbags and jewelry, but it wasn't until she discovered Spoonflower that Lisa really found her stride!

Lisa launched her blog, *Tango & James*, in 2008, and began selling her designs on Etsy and at her local handmade market in Canberra, Australia. Her strong passion for interior design is evident in her own home, which has been featured in Australia's *Home Beautiful* magazine.

Lisa describes her style as bold in pattern and fun in color: "I always hope my style brings out a smile... I have a strong love of bold pattern and mixing it up! Kate Spade does this in a way I adore. I grew up despising curtains because I had never seen ANY that I liked—that was until I spotted Jonathan Adler's interiors. I love the way his curtains look so architectural; like they are part of the decor. I love the way the poles and rings are seen, and the curtain panels aren't just gathered up or festooned. I finally saw how great curtains can be, and I wanted to use my own prints in that way."

Lisa's "Bannisters" curtains—the pattern was inspired by turned wood—adorn the windows in her living room, and she admits they are her absolute favorite. "I love the silhouette, and the repetition of them as a stripe... the curtains

> *"Digital fabric prints are so crisp and perfect, with lively color and no mess!"*

in this room add a much-needed graphic element and draw focus away from the TV!"

When it comes to curtain making, Lisa says she pretty much makes it up as she goes along. I think we can all agree that she clearly has a natural talent!

**TANGO & JAMES**
www.tangoandjames.blogspot.com
www.spoonflower.com/profiles/
ninaribena

**LIVES**
Canberra, Australia

**WINDOW TREATMENT STYLE**
Unlined curtains

**FABRIC USED**
"Bannisters" by Tango & James

**SIMILAR TUTORIALS**
Basic Unlined Curtains, pages 72–73
Using Heading Tape, pages 94–97

# Blinds
## Gallery

**Left:** Charlotte Rivers/Lottie Loves. **Top:** Gap Interiors/
Douglas Gibb. **Bottom:** Anna DeBois/Peaceful Happy
Home. **Opposite:** Gap Interiors/Bruce Hemming.

# CHAPTER 7
## Valances and Decorative Treatments
# Overview

Valances and pelmets add an extra dimension to your window dressings. They can be used to hide unsightly curtain hardware or be the main focal point for your window—or perhaps the only focal point! As with many interiors projects, the valance comes in and out of fashion. Valances were once overly fussy, frilly affairs, and once again that style is coming back. Ruffles are also everywhere! I've included a tutorial for ruffles along with a couple of basic pleating techniques; pleats and ruffles you can attach to your curtains and blinds wherever you see fit. Other tutorials include making a plywood pelmet and a soft, scalloped-edge valance. Making pelmets is a lot of fun, and don't be daunted by power tools—they are your friends!

**Opposite:** Vanessa Schafer/Vanessa Schafer Designs

# Tutorial
# Pleats

Pleats give a structured fullness to curtains, and sometimes also add a sense of movement. Press the pleats for a sharp, Issey Miyake vibe, or leave them to hang softly for a more casual look. Use them when making a valance, a curtain heading, or a bottom border. Play around with proportion and pattern. Try adding a contrasting panel of fabric to the inside of the pleats for a flash of color.

## YOU WILL NEED

- Fabric
- Sewing machine
- Ruler
- Different colored markers
- Pins
- Iron

For both the box and knife pleat tutorials, I'm marking the folding and positioning points of the fabric by the industry standard. For your project, I'd suggest using different colored markers for each. I'm also marking on the reverse of the fabric, but if you prefer, you can mark the points on the right side of the fabric using a vanishing fabric marking pen. Referring to the box pleat diagram (opposite) and the knife pleat diagram (on page 126), **A** is the positioning point and **B** is the folding point.

## BOX PLEATS

Box pleats look complicated, but they're pretty simple to make by hand. In this example the pleats are 2in (5cm) wide and touching, and you will need three times the finished width of the fabric. Hem and stitch the lengths of fabric before pleating, and make sure your measuring and marking is accurate. If you want to make an inverted box pleat, simply turn the fabric around.

**1.** On the reverse of the fabric, mark the positioning point for your pleat (A). This will be the middle of the finished pleat. Mark another positioning point 6in (15cm) along from the first. Continue along the width of fabric.

**2.** Mark the folding points (B) 2in (5cm) on either side of the positioning points. Fold and press along each folding point with the fabric right sides together.

**3.** Bring the two folding points on either side of the positioning point together. They will now butt up to each other along the positioning point. Turn the fabric over and press.

**4.** Pin and then machine stitch the pleats together along the top of the fabric.

---

**TIP**
Before you start, make a diagram of your pleats, including the measurements. From this, you can work out fabric quantities. Make the pleats using some scrap fabric first to check the finished look.

## Box pleat front/with space

**4**

**2**

**3**

## Finished item

# Tutorial
# Pleats *continued*

## KNIFE PLEATS

Knife pleats all face in the same direction. You'll need at least three times the finished width of the fabric. In this example, each fold is 2in (5cm) wide. Hem and stitch the lengths of fabric before pleating.

**1.** Mark a positioning point on the reverse of the fabric (A). This will be the fold position of the finished pleat. Continue to mark this position along the width of the fabric, 6in (15cm) apart.

**2.** Mark the folding points (B) 4in (10cm) to the right of each positioning point. Fold and iron along these points, right sides together.

**3.** Bring the folding point to meet the positioning point on its left, which is 4in (10cm) away. Pin in place.

**4.** Turn the fabric over to reveal the pleats. Machine stitch together along the top of the fabric.

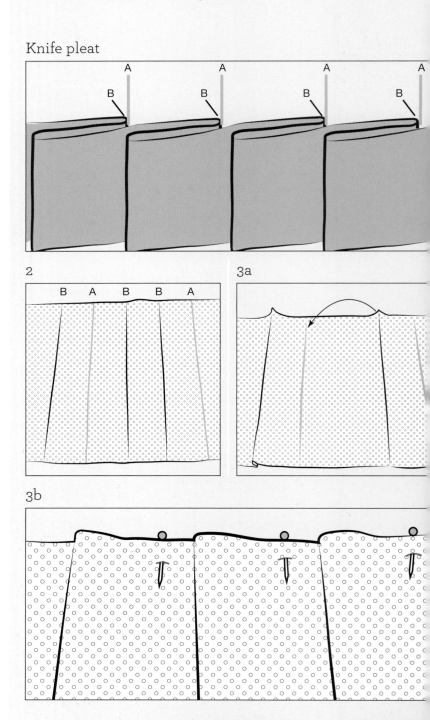

Knife pleat

2

3a

3b

**Opposite:** Gap Interiors/Tria Giovan

# Tutorial
# Ruffles

It appears we're in the middle of a ruffle renaissance, with the Anthropologie ruffled Flamenco shower curtain sending waves of DIY hysteria across the blogging community. As with most soft furnishing projects, there are several techniques for making ruffles. If you're intending to wrap your house in ruffles, it might be worth investing in a ruffler foot for your sewing machine. It makes even ruffles of various sizes and can also make the ruffle while at the same time attaching it to the curtain—magic!

Below is my favored technique. Here, I'm making a ruffle that displays the right side of the fabric on each side of the ruffle. If you don't mind the wrong side of the fabric being visible on the reverse, miss out steps 2–6. After step 1, turn a hem on both long edges of the fabric so there are no visible raw edges. For fullness, you will need two to two-and-a-half times the finished width. Join any widths together before step 1. Measure the length needed for the ruffle plus a 1¼in (3cm) seam allowance. Measure the depth of the ruffle. Double this and add 1¼in (3cm) for the seam.

## YOU WILL NEED

- Ruffle fabric cut to size
- Scissors
- Sewing machine
- Strong thread
- Safety pin
- Iron
- Ironing board

**1.** Turn in a ⅝in (1.5cm) hem along both short ends of the ruffle fabric.

**2.** Fold the fabric in half along its length with right sides together, forming a sausage. Machine stitch with a ⅝in (1.5cm) seam allowance. Press the seam.

**3.** To turn out, cut a piece of thread the length of the sausage of fabric. Tie the thread to a safety pin.

**4.** Drop the safety pin down into the sausage, keeping hold of the other end of the thread.

**5.** When the safety pin reaches the opening, secure it to the hem.

**6.** Pull the thread and work the pin back up through the sausage. When completely turned out, press flat.

**7.** Cut a piece of strong thread a touch longer than the fabric. Fasten the thread to one end of the sausage with a knot and lay the thread flat, parallel to the seam. This will hold the thread in place when you come to pull the ruffles into shape.

**8.** Hold the thread straight along the length of fabric and machine a zigzag stitch over the top of the thread and down the entire length of the fabric.

**9.** Holding the unfixed end of the strong thread in one hand, use your other hand to push the fabric away from you. The ruffles will start to form. Even them out as you go. You can now attach the ruffle to a curtain panel. If you're going for a layered look, position the ruffles so that the bottom of each covers the stitching of the ruffle below, or attach the ruffle inside the leading edge of the curtain.

4

7

8

5

9

Finished item

6

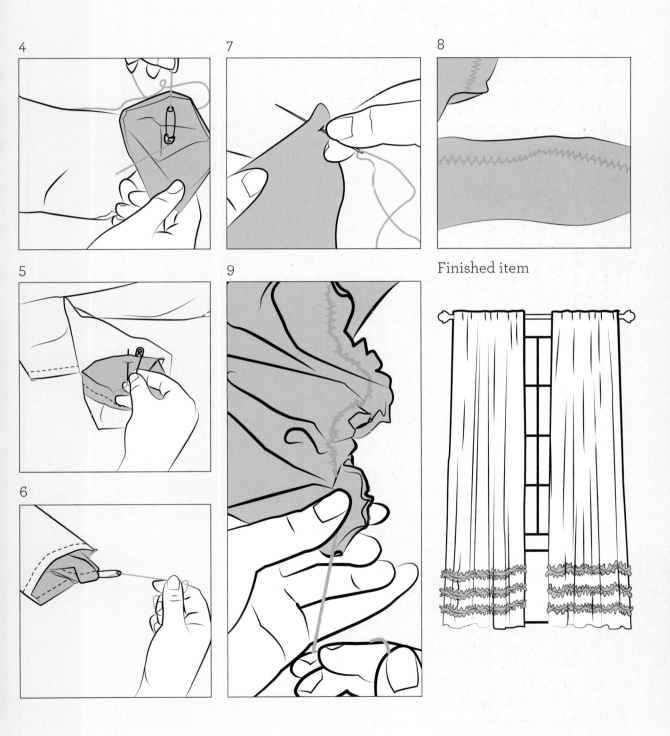

# Tutorial
# Making a Pelmet

A pelmet is a decorative feature that sits at the top of a window. It is often used to hide curtain hardware, but works equally well as a stand-alone object. In this tutorial I'm using plywood because it is strong and lightweight. I'm mounting it with a split batten so that it can be easily removed without needing a screwdriver.

To start, measure the window. The pelmet needs to be the length of the curtain rail plus about 4in (10cm). Go to your local lumberyard. You'll need three pieces of plywood: one for the face of the pelmet, and two pieces for the sides. For the batten, buy a length of 1in x 1in (2.5cm x 2.5cm) timber at least twice the height of the pelmet.

## YOU WILL NEED
- Lightweight cardboard
- Pencil
- 3 pieces of plywood ⅜in (9mm)
- 1in x 1in (2.5cm x 2.5cm) timber for the wood batten
- Jigsaw power tool
- Sandpaper
- Wood glue
- Panel board nails
- Hammer
- Spirit level
- Clamps
- Drill and drill bit
- Screws
- Screwdriver

**1.** Decide on the finished shape for your pelmet. To make the shape symmetrical, draw half of the design on a piece of cardboard. My pelmet is 39in (99cm) wide, so the template is 19½in (50.5cm) wide. Mark the halfway point on the facing piece of plywood. Place the template on one side of the line and draw around it. Flip it over and draw the shape on the opposite side of the line.

**2.** Cut out the shape using a jigsaw. Sand any rough edges smooth.

**3.** Cut the 1in x 1in (2.5cm x 2.5cm) batten 2in (5cm) shorter than the height of the finished pelmet. Cut one for each side. Lay the battens side by side and cut each batten in half at a 45° angle. You should now have two pairs of cut battens. Make sure to label the pairs, for example, left top bottom, right top bottom, etc. It's not that crucial how accurate your cutting is, as the pieces will always marry up.

**4.** Make a line 1in (2.5cm) from the top of the side pelmets. Cover one side of the top halves of the split batten with glue and position on the side pelmets, lining up with the 1in (2.5cm) mark.

**5.** Turn over and nail the side pelmet and batten together.

**6.** Hammer a line of panel nails into the facing piece of the pelmet, but don't hammer all the way through.

**7.** Glue the edge of the pelmet side and bring the facing on top of the side panel. You will need someone to help you with this. Hammer the nails home.

**8.** Drill holes through the bottom sections of the remaining two battens. Hold the pelmet up to the wall and make sure it is level (you will need an extra pair of hands for this). On the left-hand side of the pelmet, position the bottom half of the batten under the top batten and mark around it. Repeat on the right-hand side of the pelmet.

**9.** Take the pelmet away and screw the bottom battens to the wall in the position you've marked.

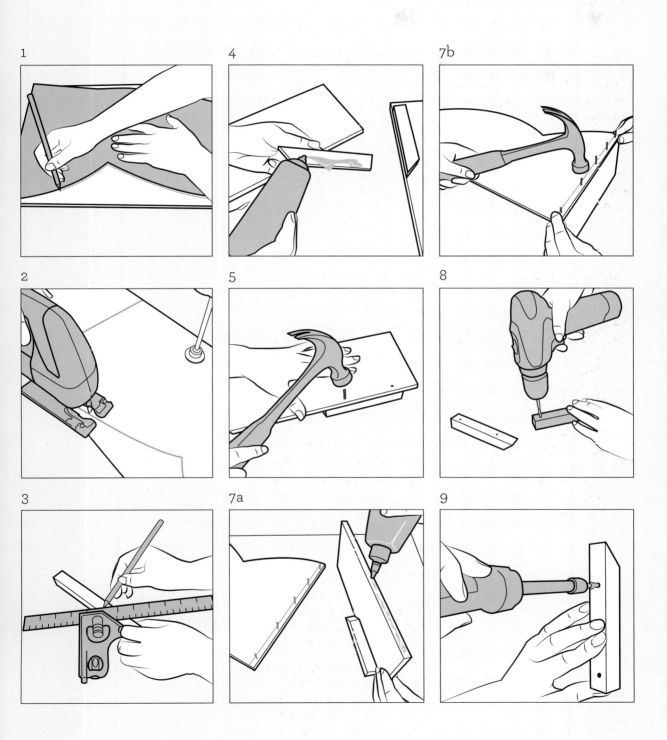

# Tutorial
# Covering a Pelmet

You've hopefully followed the pelmet-making tutorial on pages 130–131. It's a really simple process, so give it a go! If you already have a pelmet in position, remove it from the wall and give it a good dust. There are many finishes you can apply to a pelmet. You can choose to cover it in fabric or simply paint it. In this example, I'm painting the inside and edges of the pelmet, covering the front and sides in fabric, and finishing it off with a contrasting trim.

## YOU WILL NEED

- Pre-made pelmet (see pages 130–131)
- Sandpaper
- Spraypaint
- Fabric
- Trim
- Spray adhesive
- Polyester batting
- Upholstery tack strip (or a straight piece of cardboard) the length of the pelmet
- Staple gun
- Hot glue gun
- Scissors
- Craft knife
- Hammer
- 2 small panel board nails

**1.** Sand any sharp edges on your pelmet. Spray-paint the edges and interior of the pelmet.

**2.** Cut the fabric to the depth and width of the pelmet plus 4in (10cm). Cut center point notches on the top and bottom of the fabric.

**3.** Position the pelmet facedown and mark the center points at the top and bottom. Lay the fabric, wrong side up, along the top of the pelmet. Make sure the notch on your fabric lines up with the center of the pelmet. Run some tack strip or cardboard over the fabric so that the bottom of the cardboard is 1in (2.5cm) from the top of the pelmet. Staple in position.

**4.** Turn the pelmet over with the right side facing up. Spray with adhesive.

**5.** Cover with a thin layer of polyester batting. Trim the batting so that it sits about ⅜in (1cm) up from the bottom of the pelmet. If you don't trim the batting back, the staples applied in step 6 will form dimples in the fabric.

**6.** Bring the fabric back over the top of the pelmet. Smooth the fabric down from the top to the bottom of the pelmet and staple just below the cut edge of the batting.

**7.** When you are happy with how the fabric looks, trim along the bottom of the pelmet with scissors or a craft knife.

**8.** Next, attach the trim to the face of the pelmet along the bottom edge. Fold under the end of a length of trim. Position the folded end at the back of the pelmet and glue in place with the hot glue gun. Hammer a panel board nail into the fold, but don't hammer right through the trim and pelmet—the nail is just being used to hold the trim in place while you glue. Continue gluing the trim along the bottom of the pelmet. When you reach the opposite side turn the trim under, glue, and pin in place.

**9.** When the trim is completely dry, remove the panel board nails and bring the pelmet to the wall. Slot the battens on the pelmet onto the ones on the wall. Stand back and admire!

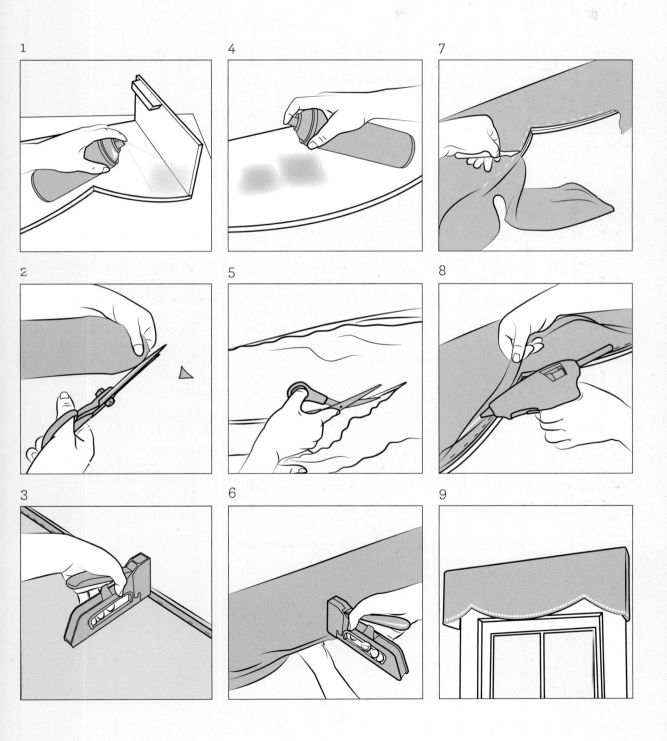

1

2

3

4

5

6

7

8

9

# Tutorial
# Piping

Piping is used in soft furnishings and upholstery to strengthen fabric joins and to give that professional "finished" look. For curtains, you can add piping to tiebacks or to valances. Play with contrasting or complementary colors, bringing some interest to the overall look.

## YOU WILL NEED

- Piping cord
- Sewing machine with a piping foot or zipper foot
- Fabric
- Matching thread
- Ruler
- Chalk

## SINGLE PIPING

**1.** Lay out your fabric and, using a ruler, mark out lengths of piping across the bias. If you don't have a piping stick, fold the end of your fabric over and line up with the selvage to make a square. The fold will give you the 45° line. Cut your length of fabric 1½in (4cm) thick.

**2.** Measure how much piping you will need and, if necessary, join lengths together. To do this, begin by squaring off both ends. Position one end of the fabric length over another, right sides facing. Mark a line across the diagonal.

**3.** Machine stitch along the mark and then trim close to the stitched line.

**4.** Turn the fabric over and, using a small ruler (or something heavy), press open the seam. If your fabric is pretty thick, or you have the time, press open with an iron. If all has gone to plan, the joins should be sitting on the wrong side of your fabric lengths.

**5.** Lay the cord centrally on the wrong side of the fabric and fold over. Keep the raw edges of the fabric together as you run the lengths through the machine. The finished length of piping will have an enclosed piece of cord on one side and two pieces of fabric for the stitching allowance on the other. The piping is now ready to attach to the border of a tieback, or perhaps along the edges of your curtains.

**TIP**
If you're making piping for tiebacks that will one day be washed, be sure to prewash the cord first.

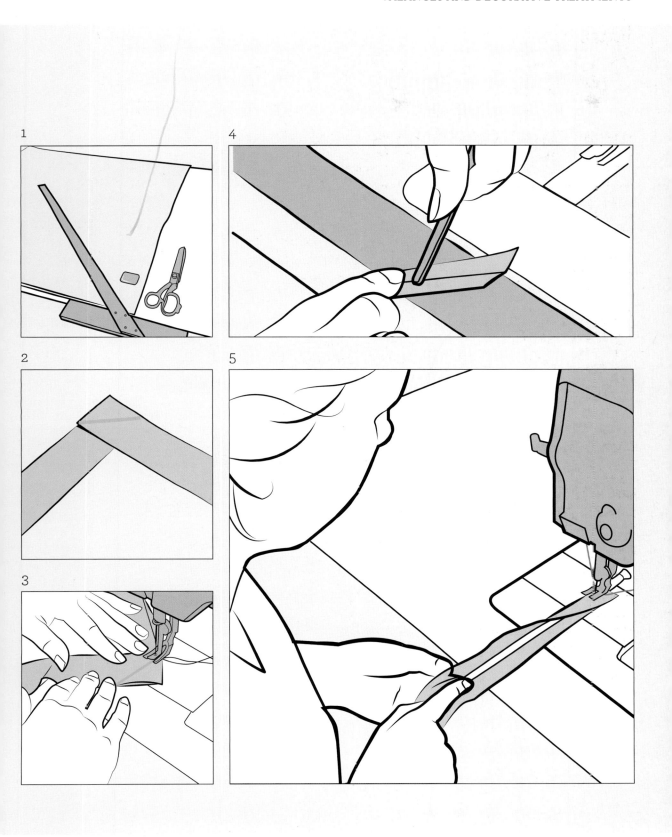

# Tutorial
# Piping *continued*

## JOINING PIPING

If you are making a traditional tieback with a piped edge detail (like in the Tieback tutorial on pages 160–161), you will need to finish your piping by joining two ends together. There are a couple of ways to join the ends—a hard way and a simple way! If your fabric is heavyweight, I'd suggest following these instructions and doing it the hard way...

**1.** Leaving roughly 2⅛in (6cm) of piping free, machine stitch your piping around the edges of the tieback. The encased cord will be facing into the tieback and the seam allowance will be in line with the outer edge of the tieback. Lay both ends of the piping over each other and mark a 1½in (4cm) overlap. Cut the overlapped piece of piping at this mark.

**2.** Open out both pieces of piping to expose the cord. Bring the two right sides of the piping fabric together. Line the end edge of the right-hand piece up with the bottom edge of the left piece and pin.

**3.** Sew across the diagonal, starting from the bottom corner of your right-hand piece and working to the top corner of your left-hand piece. Trim the excess just outside the sewn line. Open out and flatten.

**4.** Lay the joined pieces down and cut the piping so that the ends meet. Continue sewing around to encase the piping.

> **TIP**
> A quicker method of joining piping is to trim the cord, fold under one side of the fabric, wrap around the cord, and continue stitching. This method should not be used for heavyweight fabric, as the extra bulk will not be evenly spaced.

1

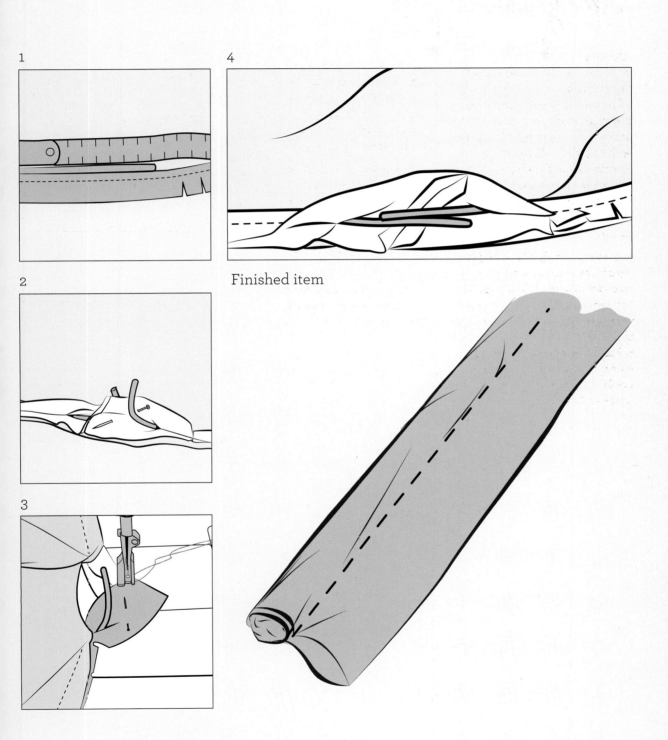

4

Finished item

# Tutorial
# Soft Valance

A valance is a soft fabric heading either hung alone or paired with blinds or curtains. These were popular in Victorian-era interior design, and appear to be making a comeback. They're perfect for concealing any unsightly hardware or can simply be used for decoration. If fixed to a pole, the soft valance will need to extend beyond the ends and not restrict the movement of the curtain or blind. It might be worth investing in a double curtain pole, which only requires one set of attachments. In this tutorial I'm making a valance with a scalloped edge and simple pole casing. This can be left flat or hung with simple gathers.

## YOU WILL NEED

- Fabric for valance front and back
- Pattern drafting paper or cardboard
- Pen
- Craft knife
- Tailor's chalk or marker
- Ruler
- Scissors
- Sewing machine
- Iron

**1.** Measure the width of your finished valance and divide by the number of scallops to give you the width for each. To make the template, draw two parallel lines, a scallop-width apart, on some pattern drafting paper or cardboard. Line up a bowl or plate between the marks and draw around it. There will be sharp joins between semicircular curves. These can be tricky to work with, as the seams are likely to pucker. A shallower curve will be easier for a beginner.

**2.** Draw a line across the shape where the curve meets the two lines. Mark the center line and cut out the template.

**3.** Select two pieces of fabric: one for the front of the valance and the other for the reverse. Cut both pieces the width of the finished valance plus a 1¼in (3cm) seam allowance. For the height, add approximately 1in (2.5cm) for the pole casing and a 1¼in (3cm) seam allowance. Depending on the size of your windows, you may need to join together some widths of fabric. To do this, lay the fabric right sides together and mark the center line. Draw a seam allowance line ⅝in (1.5cm) in from the bottom, top, and sides, then pin and sew together.

**4.** If you have an odd number of scallops, position the center line of the template on the fabric center line. The bottom should rest on the seam allowance. Draw around the template. Move along the seam allowance line and continue to draw around it. If the number of scallops is even, position one of the outside edges alongside the center line.

**5.** Draw the seam allowance around the scalloped shapes. At this point, pin the two fabrics together, close to the edge. Cut out the scalloped edge.

**6.** Machine stitch around the shape, right sides together, leaving the pole casing and about 4in (10cm) on one side open. This is to help turn the valance right side out.

**7.** Notch around the scallops. This will help ease the fabric into shape.

**8.** Turn the fabric right sides out and press. Mark the bottom of the pole pocket across the top of the valance. Machine stitch along this line to hold all the layers together.

**9.** Slip stitch the turning hole closed. Work the curtain pole through the casing and hang in place.

> **TIP**
> If you're returning the valance to the wall, visually it's a good idea to have half a scallop at both ends.
>
> At step 8, use a blunt knife inside the valance to push out the scallop shape while pressing.

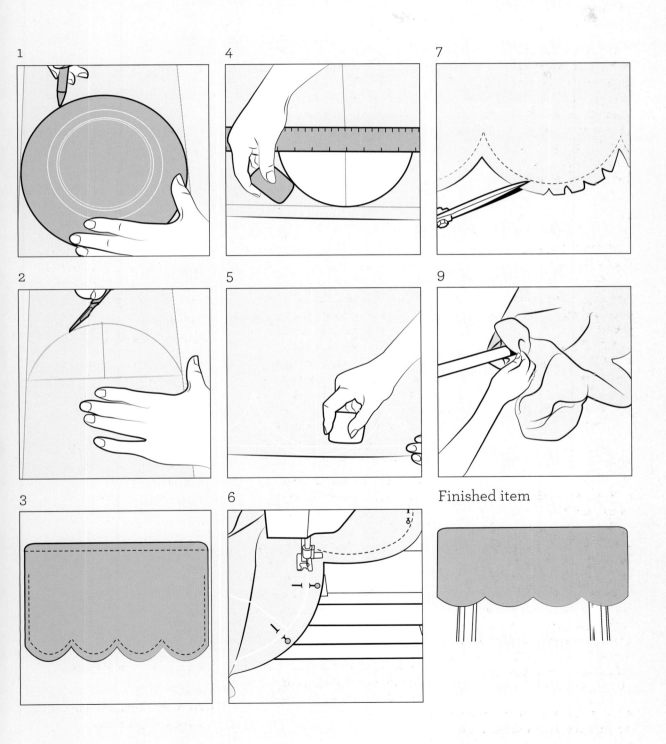

1

2

3

4

5

6

7

9

Finished item

# Tutorial
# Decorative Borders

Decorative borders can be designed as part of a curtain and planned and incorporated into its construction. Think twice before throwing out your undersized vintage finds—by attaching a border, you can extend and enliven an existing curtain panel. Below are two tutorials: one is an extended border using a simple fabric join, and the other uses off-the-shelf webbing (see page 142).

## YOU WILL NEED
- Curtain
- Border fabric
- Sewing machine
- Thread
- Ruler
- Tailor's chalk or vanishing marker
- Scissors

## EXTENDED BORDER

**1.** Cut a strip of fabric double the depth of border you require, plus a 1¼in (3cm) seam allowance. Mark the center line along the length of the fabric using either chalk or a vanishing marker.

**2.** Place the border strip along the bottom edge of the curtain panel, right sides together, and pin in place. Stitch with a ⅝in (1.5cm) seam allowance.

**3.** Keeping the curtain wrong side down, fold over the border strip, and press along the stitched line.

**4.** Turn the curtain over with the right side facing down. Fold and press the border along its center line with the wrong sides together—this is the bottom of your curtain.

**5.** Fold under the raw edge of the border panel by ⅝in (1.5cm). Press and either machine topstitch or slip stitch the border in place by hand.

**TIP**
Traditionally, if you are adding a border to all four edges of a curtain, start with the top and bottom borders and finish with the leading edge.

2

5

3

Finished item

4

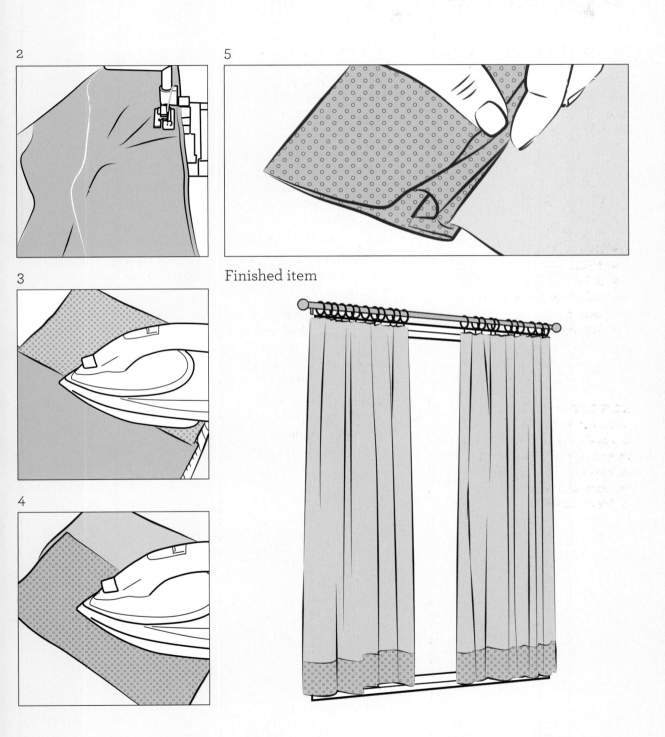

# Tutorial
# Decorative Borders continued

## YOU WILL NEED

- Curtain fabric
- Cotton webbing
- Sewing machine
- Thread
- Pins
- Iron

## COTTON WEBBING BORDER AND TIES

This is a really simple addition to a basic unlined curtain, and uses cotton webbing as both a decorative border and a tie to attach to the pole. Cotton webbing is a flat woven strip, typically with a herringbone pattern. It comes in many different sizes, so go for one that feels in keeping with the proportions of your finished curtain (in this case I have decided to use 1³⁄₈in/35mm cotton webbing).

As this curtain is held to the pole by ties, the distance from the curtain pole to the top of the finished curtain can be easily adjusted. Once you've decided on the drop length, you can cut your curtain panel fabric to the finished width and drop length, adding a 1¼in (3cm) seam allowance all round (¼in/6mm less than your tape width).

**1.** Lay the fabric right-side up, turn and press 1¼in (3cm) hems, right sides together, all the way round.

**2.** For the ties, cut the webbing to double the required length and fold in half. If in doubt, make them longer—you can always trim after an initial test hang. Position a folded tie at either end of the curtain and space evenly along the curtain header. Make sure they sit within the 1¼in (3cm) hem area. Pin in place.

**3.** Lay strips of cotton webbing over the side hems of the curtain, stopping short by ³⁄₈in (1cm) at each end. Pin in place and topstitch neatly.

**4.** Repeat the process for the top and bottom hems, but this time turn the ends of the webbing under by ³⁄₈in (1cm) to form neat corners. The tape at the top of the curtain will secure the tie tops in place. Machine stitch together. Hang the curtains and tie as desired. Once you are happy with the length of the ties, you can trim and finish neatly to the desired length.

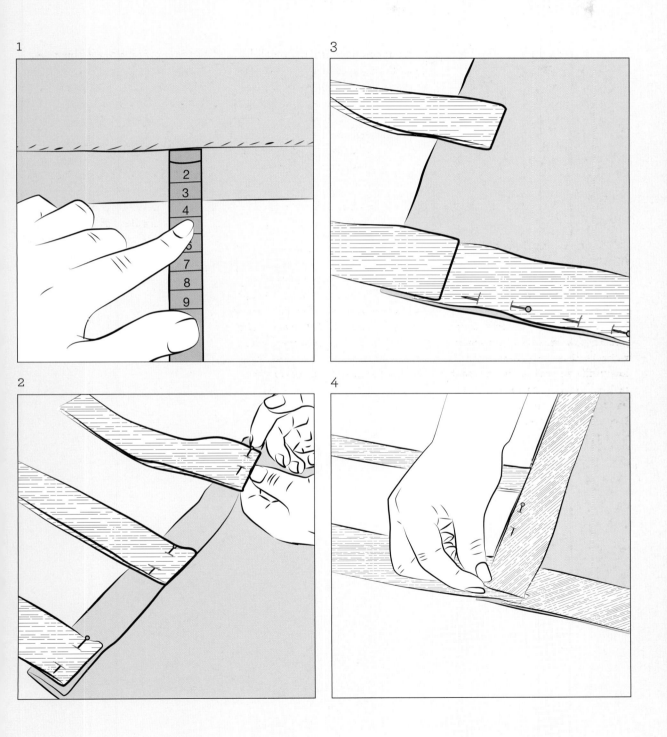

# Tutorial
# Trims

The addition of a trim can really transform the look of a curtain or blind. There are plenty to choose from—braids, fringes, beads, pompoms, lace, and feathers—the list goes on. Don't feel limited by the selection of notions sold specifically for curtains. Choose trims with good structure that will attach to the leading edges of your curtains and allow you to see them in their full glory. Feathers and braids hold their shape well, and ruffles made from a stiff fabric like linen are also a good option. Fringes and trims are perfect attached to the bottom of blinds.

In many cases, the trim and its border are designed to be visible. To attach, make up the curtain in the usual way and machine stitch in place. If the border is very narrow, pin and stitch by hand. In this example I'm concealing the border in the bottom of a Roman blind, but this method of attaching the trim would be the same for curtains. If you're following the Roman Blinds tutorial on pages 110–115, follow step 1, and turn in the side hems but not the bottom hem. From that point, continue to follow the instructions below.

**YOU WILL NEED**
- Trim
- Curtain or blind panel
- Tailor's chalk
- Sewing machine
- Thread
- Scissors
- Pins
- Ruler
- Iron

**1.** Make a note of the measurement between the base of the trim and where the visible element starts. This will be your cutting allowance for step 2 and the seam allowance for step 6. If the border is narrower than ⅜in (1cm), machine stitch a length of cotton webbing or similar to the trim to extend the selvage.

**2.** Mark the finished drop point on the main blind panel. Add on the measurement from step 1, draw a line, and trim the fabric.

**3.** With the blind right-side up, pin the trim along the bottom edge. The decorative edge of the trim will be facing into the blind.

**4.** Cut a piece of fabric for the facing. It needs to be the width of the finished blind, plus extra for side turnings. If you're making a Roman blind, the depth of the facing needs to be 4in (10cm), plus the seam allowance from step 1.

**5.** Place the facing right-side down on top of the trim, raw edges together. Remove the pins, and re-place to hold all three layers together. The order should be: main fabric, trim, facing.

**6.** Stitch all three together with the seam allowance calculated in step 1.

**7.** Turn back the facing so that the right side is upward on the reverse of the blind. Press to make the bottom line of the blind crisp while pulling gently on the trim. This will help bring the seam out. If the trim is not being inserted into a lined curtain or blind, fold, press, and stitch the raw edge of the facing to the main fabric.

**TIP**
Some trims can fray easily when cut, so consider applying a liquid seam sealant or hot glue to the raw edge. For others, machine zigzag or hand stitch the ends in place.

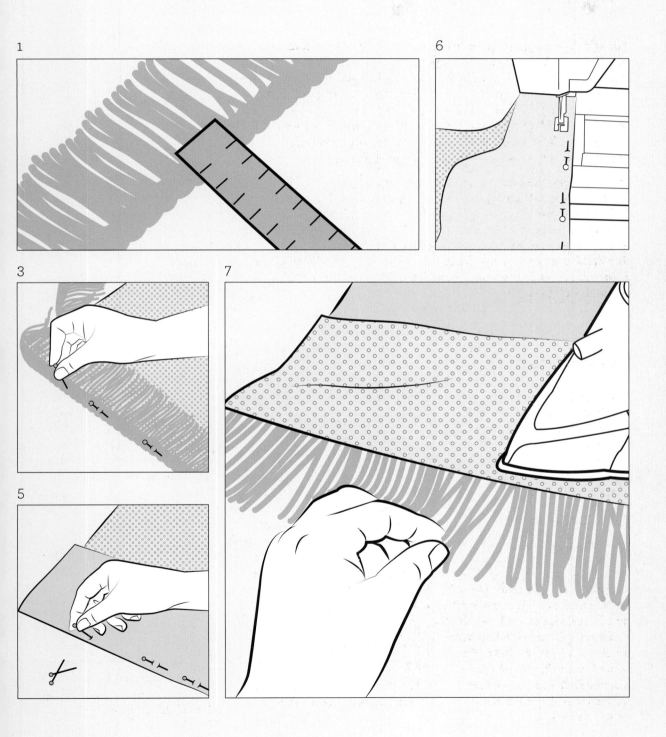

# Case Study
# Kristine Franklin, The Painted Hive

Kristine is a passionate home enthusiast and a talented self-taught interior decorator. Her blog, *The Painted Hive,* is all about decorating on a budget. For this project, Kristine wanted to turn a disused room into a home office. A practical, affordable and attractive solution was needed to both diffuse the summer sun and shield against the winter chill.

Kristine's solution was to buy a standard roller blind: "They are cheap, effective, light blocking, climate controlling, easy to use and readily available, though on the downside, they aren't particularly pretty." To hide the roller mechanism, Kristine decided to build a pelmet and cover it with a ticking valance. "I deliberately chose a neutral ticking because it's so versatile. It's able to complement a myriad of different interiors."

The roller blind was installed above and to the exact width of the window architrave. For the pelmet, Kristine measured the window at its widest point and added roughly 2in (5cm) for a slight overhang. Another offcut piece of timber was glued and screwed to the side of the pelmet. The screws were countersunk and the holes filled and painted to match the window.

Kristine made two identical valances to sit next to each other. A dowel pocket was folded and stitched along the bottom of the panel, with a slightly narrower piece of dowel fed through.

Both finished valances were then stapled to the top of the pelmet. If you have no staples or tacks to

> *The combination of timeless ticking fabric, natural linen ribbon, and rustic timber buttons helps with the overall unpretentious feel, and the subtle curves impart a gentle softness.*

**THE PAINTED HIVE**
www.thepaintedhive.net

**LIVES**
Melbourne, Australia

**WINDOW TREATMENT STYLE**
Roll-up window valance over a roller blind

**FABRIC/MATERIALS USED**
Ticking
Twill tape
Timber buttons

**SIMILAR TUTORIALS**
Making a Pelmet, pages 130–131

hand, Kristine suggests using Velcro: "This may be handy if you have plans to take the valance down frequently or if you like the idea of creating additional valance panels in different fabrics that can be easily interchanged!"

To hold the rolls in place, Kristine cut twill tape to the finished valance length plus a few inches extra. The ends of the tape were then turned, machine stitched, and held together with buttons. With the valance rolled to the desired length, Kristine passed the buttoned tapes over the pelmet. L-brackets were positioned above the roller blind and the pelmet lifted into position.

# Valances and Decorative Treatments
# Gallery

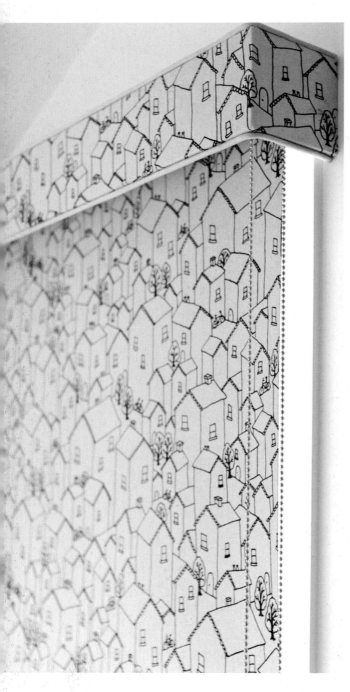

**Left:** Lara Cameron/Ink & Spindle. **Top:** Amelia Warren/House Pretty Blog. **Bottom:** Gap Interiors/Douglas Gibb. **Opposite.** Megan Duesterhaus/The Homes I Have Made.

# CHAPTER 8

## Finishing Touches

# Overview

Now you have basic curtain and blind making skills under your belt, it's just as simple to apply decorations. Trimmings can be added during the making process, or used to freshen up an existing curtain. With so many trimmings available, selecting the one you want to use will be the trickiest part! You can use trimmings as a border or to add length and interest to an old pair of curtains, or if you fancy getting a little more hands-on, think about stenciling or dyeing fabric. Cut your own stencils or search for ready-made designs online. Also have fun with dye—I've included a tutorial for ombré dyeing, but also think about using wax to create pattern in a batik style. Get creative!

**Opposite:** Gap Interiors/Douglas Gibb

# Customizing Curtains and Blinds

Adding your own unique twist to ready-made curtains and blinds, or simply customizing your own fabric, is immensely satisfying. Be playful with whatever technique you employ and find inspiration in your surroundings. Brainstorm and keep a sketchbook handy. Try to come up with unexpected ideas and experiment with materials. Below are some ideas to get you started.

## BLOCK AND LINOLEUM PRINTING

A linoleum print is not far removed from the classic potato print. It's suited to line-heavy designs rather than flat blocks of color, and the finished print has a handmade, textural quality. Linoleum is available as a flat sheet or ready-mounted on a woodblock, and is cut with a special linoleum-cutting tool. Look out for stores selling starter kits rather than diving in and investing in an array of cutters.

Freehand-draw or trace your image (reversed) onto the linoleum. If possible, clamp the linoleum down so you have more control, and keep both hands behind the blade when cutting. Heating the lino slightly will make it easier to cut. With careful positioning and marking, it is possible to produce repeated patterns. Experiment with different colors by offsetting the linoleum on the next print, but check the transparency of the ink and how the colors mix before committing to your final fabric.

## DIGITAL FABRIC PRINTING

Digital fabric printing enables you to print multiple colors, so you can be as creative as you like in terms of color and pattern. Online companies specializing in digital fabric printing are popping up everywhere. Some offer a small-run service, which is great if you only need enough fabric for a pair of curtains or a blind. Creating a unique design for your soft furnishings has become so simple and you don't need to be a computer genius, as some companies even offer a design and setup service.

## SCREEN-PRINTING

All the tools and chemicals you need to screen-print at home can be bought online or from large art and craft suppliers. You can also make a simple print without the use of chemicals—simply cut a paper stencil and place it between the screen and fabric, then pull some ink across the screen with a squeegee. The ink will only transfer to the fabric through the open area of the stencil. If you opt to use chemicals and expose the screen, you'll need somewhere completely dark for the light-sensitive screen to dry, and you'll also need the correct wattage bulb for exposing. Whichever method you choose, test the print on a scrap piece of fabric first—it might be that you need to pull the squeegee over the screen more than once for a decent print.

Taking a course in screen printing is by far the best way to learn the basics because of the tips, advice, and inspiration you get from working with other printmakers.

## EMBELLISHING

Traditional embroidery is the act of decorating fabric using a needle and thread, but these days there's no need to be restricted. Even the most basic sewing techniques can change the feel of a fabric.

Appliqué, meaning "applied," has been around for centuries. The process involves cutting out a shape in one fabric and stitching it to another. If you're an appliqué novice, start with a simple, basic shape. Unless you're using felt, some fabrics will fray once they are cut. The best way to avoid this is to use the sheet variety of fusible web. It comes with a paper side and a shiny side, the latter being covered in glue. Make sure whichever brand you are using is suitable for machine stitching. Draw your shapes onto the paper side of the web, lay the shiny side onto the reverse of the fabric, and press. Cut out the shapes, remove the paper from the web to expose the glue, lay the glued side down on the main fabric, and press again. Now stitch around the perimeter of the design with zigzag or straight stitch. Rather than reverse-stitching at the beginning and end, simply pull the threads to the reverse of the fabric and tie off. To do this, turn the fabric over and pull on the bobbin thread. This will start to bring the needle thread through the fabric. Use a pin to pull the thread fully through and tie off.

**Opposite:** Claudia Roberts/Runaway Coast

# Tutorial
# Stenciling

I love printmaking. Even the humble potato can deliver a fantastic print. For me, part of the satisfaction of printing is in the simple cutting of the lino or stencil. If you're in a hurry or don't trust your cutting skills, there are hoards of stencils and stamps available in stores or online. For this tutorial I'm cutting a stencil using a sheet of acetate. Frisket film is great for more complicated designs, as the tacky back holds the stencil in place. Cardboard is good for large and simple designs, but paper is really only suitable for a one-off print.

## YOU WILL NEED
- Acetate or frisket film
- Permanent marker
- Cutting mat
- Craft knife
- Paper
- Ruler
- Curtain or blind
- Masking tape
- Fabric paint
- Roller tray
- Roller or stencil dabber
- Scrap piece of fabric for testing
- Plastic sheet
- Absorbent paper

**1.** Draw out your design on paper. Place the acetate or film over the design and tape down to hold in place. Trace your design using a permanent marker.

**2.** Cut out the shape using your craft knife.

**3.** Lay a sheet of plastic on your work surface. Cover this with some absorbent paper.

**4.** Press the curtain or blind fabric flat. Lay your curtain or blind on top of the paper. If the stencil relies heavily on a repeating pattern or is very straight, mark the positioning with some masking tape.

**5.** Pour the fabric paint into the roller tray. Load the roller with paint and offload in the tray. To do this, repeatedly roll the roller in one direction in the tray. The paint will even out over the surface of the roller.

**6.** Hold the stencil down with one hand and roll over it with the paint roller. The paint will dispense differently depending on the density of the roller itself and the sort of fabric you are using. You may need to repeat or apply more pressure as you go for better coverage.

**7.** Carefully remove the stencil and reposition, applying with paint again, and follow the paint instructions for drying.

> **TIP**
> Mark the corners of your design on the acetate. This will help line everything up as you move along the fabric.

1

4

7

Finished item

2

5

3

6

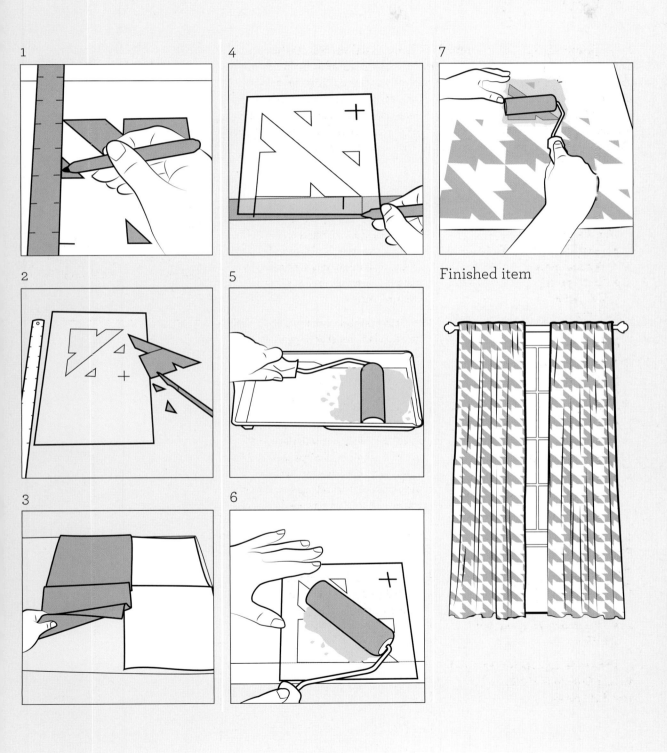

# Tutorial
# Ombré Dyeing

Dyeing fabric is easy, and changing the color of fabric can dramatically update your curtains and blinds. Before committing to yards of potentially expensive fabric for a new project, research how the fabric will work with the dye. Cotton, linen, and viscose generally take color well, while synthetics will give lighter results or not take the dye at all. If in doubt, check with the fabric supplier. Some major dye manufacturers offer a service that allows you to send fabric samples off for testing. If the fabric is already colored, adding dye will produce a new color. Here are a few examples of color mixing results:

**Red + blue = purple**
**Blue + yellow = green**
**Red + yellow = orange**

## YOU WILL NEED
- Curtains
- Fabric dye
- Salt
- A big bucket
- Some kind of holding device
- Rubber gloves
- Mixing implement

As a general rule, you will need commercial dye, salt, and warm and cold water. Warm salty water opens up the fibers in the fabric and helps the dye to be absorbed. Cold water halts the dyeing process at the desired point. Different dyes have their own instructions for use, so follow these for the best results, and always use the correct amount of dye for the weight of fabric.

Ombré or dip dyeing will require a touch more effort, but the results can be fantastic and create a more bespoke finish. Whichever dyeing technique you employ, there are few things you need to consider.

With ombré, setting up a dyeing stand is paramount. The fabric will need to be suspended above the bucket of dye at various heights during the process. I've hung the fabric over a pole between two stepladders. If the fabric panel is wide, it's best to use a wide and deep tray. A plastic window box (without holes) is ideal. If you are limited to a bucket, make sure there aren't any folds in the fabric, otherwise you could end up with patchy areas.

**1.** Wash the curtain at the correct temperature. Mix a packet of fabric dye with warm water in a small pitcher.

**2.** Measure roughly 1½ gallons (6 liters) of warm water into a bucket. Pour a quarter of the mixed dye into the bucket. Pour in the salt and mix everything together well.

**3.** Wrap the fabric around a pole and pin in place. I've used a cardboard fabric roll. You could try using a broom handle or wood dowel. Submerge the fabric in the dye and leave for about 15 minutes.

**4.** Move the pole up the ladder and add another quarter of the dye to the bucket. Repeat this process for however many stages you'd like. I like to use a slightly darker but matching dye for the very last shade to add a touch more contrast.

**5.** When you are happy with the effect, remove the fabric from the dye and rinse in cold water until the water runs clear. Hang out to dry away from direct sunlight. Wash with detergent at the correct temperature.

2

4

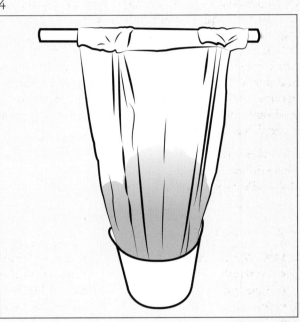

3

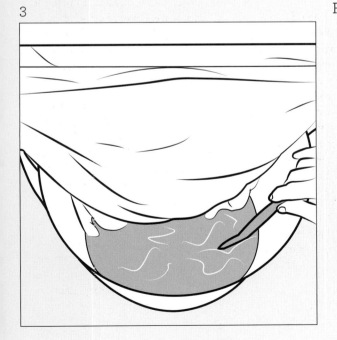

Finished item

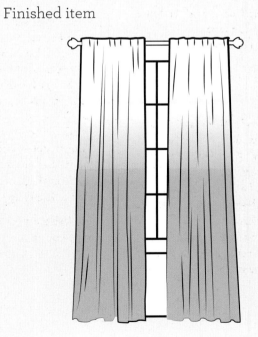

# Tutorial
# Cords and Tassels

Cords and tassels can be pretty extravagant things, adorned with beads, knots, and multiple colored threads. I prefer the simplicity of the handmade tassel—as long as it is good and plump, I'm happy. The following is a tutorial for making twisted cord and a basic tassel. Use a soft cord for the tassel, as this will help to aid the way it hangs.

## YOU WILL NEED - TWISTED CORD

- 2 x equal lengths of 6-strand cord

## YOU WILL NEED - TASSEL

- Cord
- Twisted cord
- Cardboard
- Scissors

## TWISTED CORD

**1.** Bring the ends of the cord together and tie a knot. You will now have a loop.

**2.** Put a pencil or skewer at one end and a hooked object at the other. This could be the clip on a pen cap, for example. I'm using a curtain hook.

**3.** Tape both ends of the pencil to a tabletop.

**4.** Pull the thread taut and begin to twist tightly. Eventually the thread will start to double up. When it does, twist a few more times. Take hold of the middle of the cord and bring the hook down to the pencil or skewer. The thread will twist itself together. You may need to work the twisting a little. When you are happy with the twist, tie off the ends. Remove the pencil and clip.

## TASSEL

**1.** Cut a piece of cardboard twice the length of your finished tassel. Wrap the cord around the cardboard multiple times. Keep the cord tight, but not so tight that you can't remove the cardboard.

**2.** Lay a piece of thread on a table. Remove the wrapped cord from the cardboard and place on the center of the thread. Position the twisted cord in the center point and tie together with the thread.

**3.** Cut through the cord loops at one end and bring down to meet the opposite end. Cut through the second set of loops. Tease the thread so that it covers the knotted end of the twisted cord.

**4.** Cut another long piece of cord. Make a loop in one end. Hold this against the side of the tassel, near the top. Begin to wrap the cord around the sides and over to the loop to prevent the thread coming loose. Wrap as many times as you like. Tie off the end and slip the loose threads into the tassel.

**5.** Using your fingers, comb through the tassel to make it neat and even. Trim the ends if necessary.

## TWISTED CORD

1

## TASSEL

1

4

3

2

5

4

3

Finished item

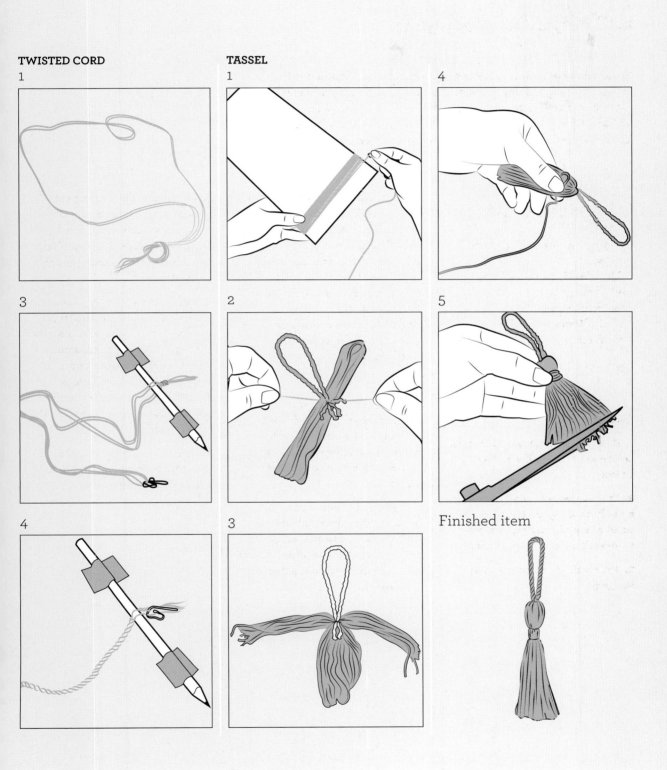

# Tutorial
# Tiebacks

Tiebacks hold curtains away from windows, either for letting in light or for decoration. Traditionally, they are made from matching fabric, but they don't have to be. Think about using ready-made items like cord, chains, or belts—I've even seen door handles and teacups used! Play with pattern and color contrasts. Sometimes, however, simplicity is best.

## YOU WILL NEED

- Piping cord and fabric (or ready-made piping)
- Fabric for the tieback
- Fabric for the reverse of the tieback
- Fusible interfacing
- Pattern drafting paper
- Pencil
- Tailor's chalk
- Sewing machine
- Piping foot or zipper foot
- Scissors
- Thread

Hang the curtains before making the tiebacks. That way, you'll get a much better idea of the window treatment as a whole. There is a theory about working in thirds—positioning the tie two-thirds of the way down the curtain gives a more balanced feel—but you may disagree. To work out the length and shape of the tieback, wrap some fabric around the curtain and measure. When you are sure of the tieback's position, attach a hook to the wall in line with the outside edge of the curtain. In the following tutorial I am going to make a traditional tieback that combines a few different techniques, including working with templates, piping, and interfacing.

**1.** Draw out a template on the pattern paper for one half of the tieback, adding a ⅝in (1.5cm) seam allowance, and cut it out.

**2.** Fold the main fabric in half, right side out, and position the leading edge of the template along the fold. Mark around the shape with tailor's chalk and cut it out. Repeat the process for the reverse fabric.

**3.** Make up some piping in your chosen fabric (see pages 134–135 for instructions on how to make piping). Make sure the piping is cut on the bias to help ease it around the shape of the tieback.

**4.** Snip the edges of the piping—this will help to ease it around the corners of the tieback. Lay the piping on the right side of the fabric, with the raw edges of the tieback and piping matched together. Position so that the ends of the piping are at the bottom of the tieback and pin in place. Using a piping or zipper foot on the sewing machine, stitch together. When you reach the piping's ends, join them and continue stitching (see pages 134–135 for information on joining piping).

**5.** Cut one piece of fusible interfacing for each tieback. It will need to sit just within the seam line. Position the interfacing on the wrong side of the fabric and iron in place.

**6.** Sandwich the piping with the reverse fabric so that the right sides are together, with the interfacing in the middle. Machine stitch, leaving a small opening for turning out. Sew with the previously piped section uppermost, so that you can see the original line of stitching. You will need to get the next line of stitching closer to the piping this time.

**7.** Clip around the seam allowance and press. Turn the right sides out and then press again. Slip stitch the opening closed.

**8.** If you need to conceal the hardware, position a curtain ring on the outside of the tieback, on the end that finishes behind the curtain. Attach another ring to the wrong side of the opposite end of the tieback and use a buttonhole stitch to secure in place. Wrap the tieback around the curtain and slip the rings over the wall hook.

4

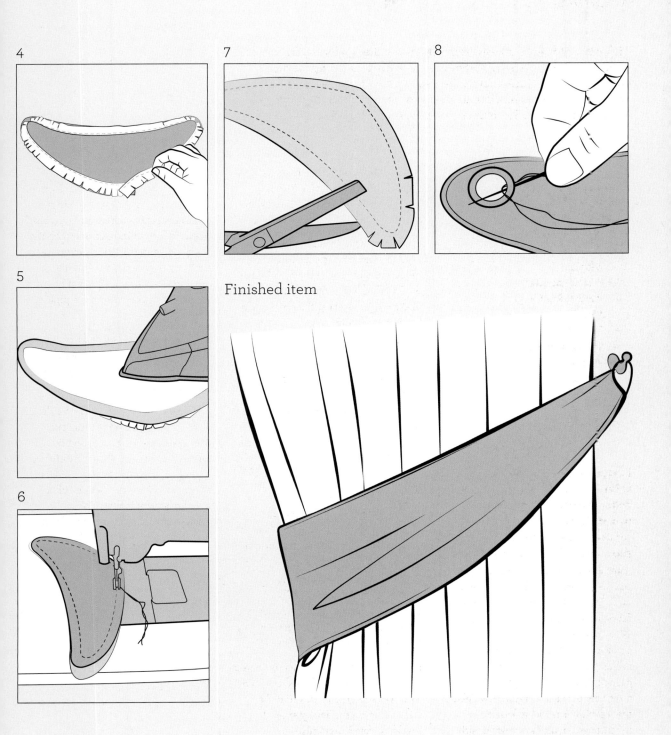

7

8

5

Finished item

6

# Case Study
# Nancy Purvis, Owen's Olivia

Nancy Purvis lives in Raleigh, North Carolina, with her husband Matt and their 3-year-old son Owen. Her spare time is spent dabbling in various creative ventures and sharing them on her blog, *Owen's Olivia*. Nancy is a lover of thrifting, design, pattern, fabric, and DIY—and is a self-confessed chevron freak!

New curtains were top of Nancy's list when it came to converting a guest bedroom into Owen's room. Although a competent sewer, Nancy decided to customize some Ikea curtains rather than make her own: "I needed something fun and playful (but not too baby-like) that blocked out light." Nancy planned to paint her favorite chevron pattern onto the curtains, but wasn't sure it would even be possible. While researching her idea she came across an article in *Better Homes & Gardens* magazine offering tips and advice for anyone wanting to paint onto fabric. She picked out four latex paint colours from Lowe's. As Nancy explains, "Latex paint is cheap, and there are tons of colors." Her next mission was to plan the pattern and painting process. Nancy opted for a method posted on the *Kristen F. Davis Designs* blog. "I was happy to read her tutorial because my first and only attempt was the right attempt, so I didn't waste any time or money."

Nancy began by dividing the curtain into four sections—one for each color—taping and painting each section one at a time. Starting at the curtain's hemline, Nancy marked out a series of V-shapes along the width of the curtain using a roofing square and some tape. Keeping a perfect

> *Hard work aside, painting these curtains is incredibly easy to do! ANYONE can paint these curtains and make them look custom. You can even take this process and do a completely different design. The sky is the limit.*

right angle is key to the success of the pattern, so using the square seemed an obvious choice. She also used 2in (5cm) tape to mark the spacing between the chevrons—2in (5cm) chevron, 2in (5cm) gap.

Once the first section of tape was in place, it was time to paint. Before diving in, brush in hand, Nancy suggests pressing along the edges of the tape to ensure the finished painted line will look crisp. "One thing

I learned from this is to not include the stitching in the design. Overall, I am very pleased with the end result!" Not surprisingly, the popular *Remodelaholic* blog invited Nancy to share her tutorial with their readers too.

Nancy swears that these curtains are the end of chevrons in her home. Well, apart from a cushion or two!

**OWEN'S OLIVIA**
www.owensolivia.blogspot.com

**LIVES**
Raleigh, North Carolina, USA

**WINDOW TREATMENT STYLE**
Faux ombré chevron curtains

**FABRIC USED**
Readymade Ikea curtains

**SIMILAR TUTORIALS**
Customizing Curtains and Blinds, pages 152–153
Ombré Dyeing, pages 156–157

# Finishing Touches
# Gallery

**Left:** Sarah Dorsey/Sarah M. Dorsey Designs.
**Top:** Mary Alice Patterson/Chateau Chic. **Bottom:** Linda
Dresselhaus. **Right:** GAP Interiors/Jonathan Gooch;
Stylist: Charlotte Love.

SECTION 3

Resources

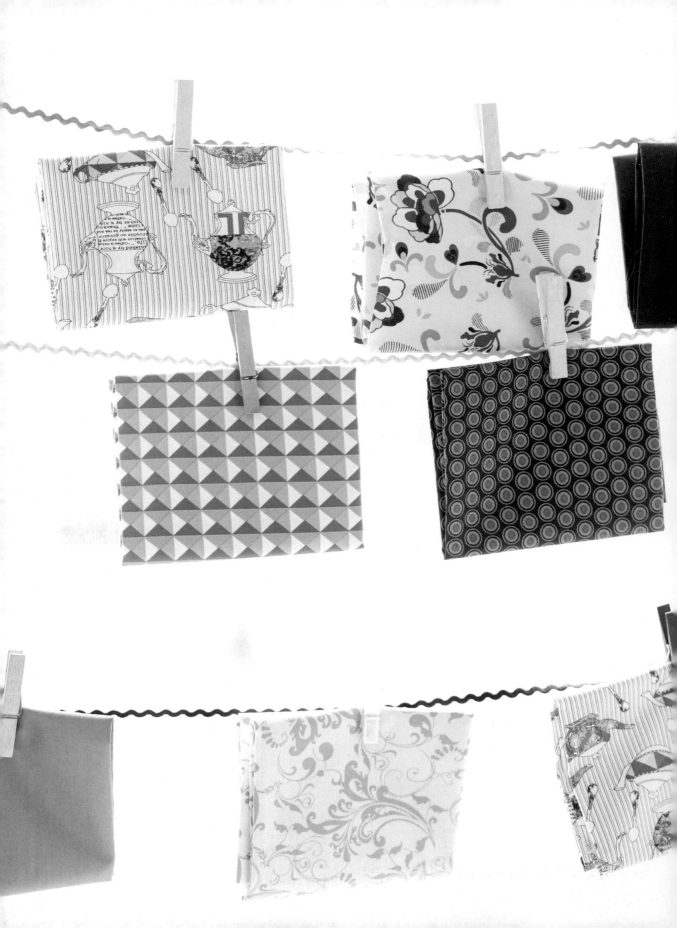

# CHAPTER 9
## Further Information
# Overview

There are so many fabric and curtain making suppliers worldwide that it's difficult to include them all. The following pages list just a few places I've come across on my travels and that have been recommended to me by other makers.

**Previous page and opposite:** Photograph by Michael Wicks

# Glossary

**BAGGING**
A technique whereby fabric is attached to lining on three sides inside out. The machined fabric is then turned right sides out.

**BIAS CUT**
The bias is a 45° cut made across the warp and weft threads of fabric. Strips of bias-cut fabric are used to make piping more flexible and easy to manipulate.

**BOLT**
A length of fabric that is wrapped around a flat piece of cardboard or tube. Sometimes the fabric will be folded in half down the length.

**CASING**
A machined channel at the top of a curtain, through which a curtain pole is inserted.

**DOUBLE HEM**
Where the bottom edge of a fabric panel is folded twice before stitching. As the name suggests, a side hem refers to the sides of the fabric.

**DRAPERY CLIPS**
A simple curtain-hanging device where metal clips and rings are clipped to the top edge of a curtain. A curtain pole is then fed through the rings.

**DRESSING**
Pleats are formed down the length of a finished hanging curtain by hand. The curtain is then brought together and pieces of fabric tied around the curtain to hold the pleats in place. If left for a day or two, the curtain will retain the folds. Do not tie too tightly!

**DROP POINT**
This is the point from which you measure your finished curtain drop. The drop point could be the eye on a curtain ring or the top of the pole.

**EYELETS**
Eyelets (or grommets) are metal or plastic rings that attach to fabric for hanging. A hole is cut in the fabric and an eyelet maker fixes the eyelet to the fabric. The curtain pole is then fed through the eyelets.

**FEED DOGS**
Feed dogs are the teeth that sit under the throat plate on your sewing machine. The teeth feed the fabric through as it is being stitched.

**FINIALS**
The removable decorative ends of a curtain pole.

**FRINGE**
A style of decorative trimming; usually a simple braid with a hanging fringe.

**FUSIBLE WEB**
Thin, ribbon-like webbing. The tape becomes sticky when hot, allowing it to join two pieces of fabric together without the need for machine or hand stitching.

**HEADING TAPE**
Heading tape (or shirring tape) is a machine-made pleating device. The tape is machine stitched onto the top of a curtain and a system of loose threads is pulled to create the pleats in the curtain. When the correct pleat formation is achieved, the loose threads are tied off, but not cut.

**LEADING EDGE**
The edge of the curtain nearest the center of the window.

**MITER**
Where corners are turned at a 45° angle for a neat finish.

**NAP**
Sometimes referred to as pile, nap is the raised surface of fabric, such as is found on velvet or corduroy. If you run your hand in the direction of the nap it is smooth; run against and it is rough. Traditionally, the nap should run down the curtain.

**NOTCH**
A V-shape that is cut into the seam allowance. Notches are used on curves so that the turned-out seam can lie flat.

**PIPING**
Welt cord covered in fabric. Use piping like a trimming along the bottom of pelmets or around tiebacks.

**PRESSER FOOT**
The presser foot holds the fabric against the feed dogs as it is being stitched.

**SEAM ALLOWANCE**
The area between the edge of the fabric and the stitched line.

**SELVAGE**
The finished outer edges of a length of fabric. The selvage was attached to the loom during production. The manufacturer and fabric name will often be printed on the selvage. It should be removed before making your curtains.

## VELCRO

Velcro (or hook and loop tape) involves one piece of tape that is covered in tiny hooks and another in tiny loops. Both pieces come together to form a strong union. Velcro comes with an adhesive backing or can be machine stitched onto fabric.

## WARP

Threads that run from top to bottom on a length of fabric.

## WEFT

Threads that run from side to side on a length of fabric.

**Right:** Gap Interiors/Rachel Whiting

# Useful Websites

## SUPPLIES

Country Curtains
www.countrycurtains.com

Drapery Sewing Supplies
www.draperysewingsupplies.com

Lowe's
www.lowes.com

## FABRIC AND TRIMMINGS

Beautiful Fabric
www.beautifulfabric.com

D'Kei Incorporated
www.dkei.org

Etsy
www.etsy.com

Fabric.com
www.fabric.com

Ikea
www.ikea.com

Jo-ann Fabric and Craft Stores
www.joann.com

Laura Ashley
www.lauraashleyusa.com

M&J Trimmings
www.mjtrim.com

Mood Fabrics
www.moodfabrics.com

Online Fabric Store
www.onlinefabricstore.net

Warehouse Fabrics
warehousefabricsinc.com

## DIGITAL FABRIC PRINTING

Advanced Digital Textiles
www.advdigitaltextiles.com

First2Print
www.first2print.com

Spoonflower
www.spoonflower.com

## LINOLEUM, STENCILS, PAINT, AND DYE

Cutting Edge Stencils
www.etsy.com/shop/
CuttingEdgeStencils

Dharma Trading
www.dharmatrading.com

Ritdye
www.ritstudio.com

U.S. Art Supply
www.usartsupply.com

## MAKERS AND BLOGS

Amanda Niederhauser
www.jedicraftgirl.blogspot.co.uk

Apartment Therapy
www.apartmenttherapy.com

Brett Bara
www.brettbara.com

Design Sponge
www.designsponge.com

Emma Kay & Co
www.emmakayandco.com

Maggi Loughran
www.maggiloughran.com

Marianne Six
www.mariannesix.com

Valerie Caldwell
www.thecaldwellproject.com

Vicky Grubb
www.somethingfine.co.uk/blog

# Contributors

Amelia Warren, House Pretty Blog
www.house-pretty.blogspot.com

Anna DeBois, Peaceful Happy Home
www.annacdebois.wordpress.com

Anne DeCocco, DeCocco Drapes
www.decoccodesign.com

Ashley McLeod, Domestic
Imperfection
www.domesticimperfection.com

Cadence Liu, Qfunvalue
www.etsy.com/shop/qfunvalue

Calle Macarone, Callemac
www.callemac.com

Charlotte Rivers, Lottie Loves
www.charlotterivers.com

Claudia Roberts, Runaway Coast
www.runawaycoast.com

Dovilé Cavina, Lovely Home Idea
www.lovelyhomeidea.com

Kristine Franklin, The Painted Hive
www.thepaintedhive.net

Lara Cameron, Ink & Spindle
www.inkandspindle.com

Linda Dresselhaus, Itsy Bits
and Pieces
www.itsy-bits-and-pieces.blogspot.com

Linda Weinstein, Calling It Home
www.callingithome.com

Lisa Barrett, Tango & James
www.tangoandjames.blogspot.com

Mary Alice Patterson, Chateau Chic
www.chateau-chic.blogspot.co.uk

Megan Duesterhaus, The Homes
I Have Made
www.thehomesihavemade.com

Melissa Braedley, Living Beautifully
DIY
www.livingbeautifullydiy.blogspot.
co.uk

Nancy Purvis, Owen's Olivia
www.owensolivia.blogspot.com

Sara Bates, Embrace My Space
www.embracemyspace.com

Sarah Dorsey, Sarah M. Dorsey
Designs
www.sarahmdorseydesigns.
blogspot.com

Sarah Langtry, Just the Bees Knees
www.justthebeesknees.com

Vanessa Schafer, Vanessa Schafer
Designs
www.vanessashafferdesigns.com

Will Taylor, Bright Bazaar
www.brightbazaarblog.com

WITH SPECIAL THANKS TO:

Brighton Sewing Centre

C&H

Gap Interiors

Michael Wicks

Price & Company

Sherry Heck

# Index